This book is dedicated to: my Mum, for not c
out; and FOX readers and Leicester City far

The Big Blue Leicester City Scrapbook

By Gary Silke, Derek Hammond, Simon Kimber & a cast of thousands...

First published in 1999 by
Juma
Trafalgar Works
44 Wellington Street
Sheffield S1 4HD
Tel. 0114 272 0915
Fax. 0114 278 6550
Email: MLacey5816@aol.com

© 1999 by G. Silke

All rights reserved. No part of this publication may be reproduced,
stored in a retrieval system, or transmitted in any form or by any means electronic,
mechanical, photocopying, recording, or otherwise,
without the prior permission of the publisher.

ISBN 1 872204 60 0

Introduction...

Brooding under the bed, piled in a cupboard, stored in the attic never to see the light of day.... we asked you to send us your sentimental City-related stash... and you did. Either brought round in person in cardboard boxes, or sent via the post in exciting looking envelopes, jiffy bags, and old style brown paper parcels... can you imagine the fun we have had? I haven't ripped off the wrapping to find the unmistakable light green Subbuteo box peering back at me for many, many years. For a few glorious weeks we had what Slade had so longingly wished for. It was Christmas every day. Then came the hard part... turning the mountain of stuff in a large pile in the middle of the carpet into a book...

This cornucopia of Leicester City junk is the result, brought to you courtesy of the people who never throw anything out, ever. For all those of you whose unfeeling parents chucked out all your stuff in a Stalinist style purge of the attic the second you left home, here it all is again. The eternal battle between houseroom and sentimentality is finally solved. This is the stuff that escaped the terrible trip to the tip... and it only takes up 1cm of your bookshelf. Show a page to your Mum and Dad, any page, and say: "These are selling for about £80 these days, and I once had five of them..." The flicker of guilty regret will make you feel better.

This collection doesn't just consist of what made it... it is also a tribute to the lost stuff:

My 1979-80 Div II Championship mug, smashed into a million pieces beyond the repairing abilities even of that glue that turns brown; Simon Smith's LCFC treasure hoard that was "...joyfully removed by a human chain of bin bag wielding relatives."; Derek Hammond's school-made City Scarf Ash Tray... long gone; Leo Tennant's 1976 City v Man United programme signed by ALL the players..... "I could have *sworn* it was in my parent's garage."; Paul Henderson's Admiral epaulettes shirt, stolen from the PE changing rooms in 1979....

Many thanks to everyone who helped with the Big Blue Scrapbook in any way...

Up the City!

Gary Silke.

The Pre-Season Tour

Before we kick off the Big Blue Scrapbook proper you have got to go on a foreign pre-season tour... every true City fanatic has at least one tucked under their belt. When life reaches the stage where trailing after City on an odyssey of low key friendlies in funny grounds was a more attractive opposition than two weeks in Spain with your loved ones.

And let's face it... before Martin O'Neill arrived it was the only way you were ever going to see City in Europe...

If you all went Vastranylland clap your hands...

Sue Williamson followed City on their tour of Finland and Sweden before what turned out to be the Second Division Championship season. This is what the locals thought of it, whatever a 'chockstart' might be...

Onsdag 25 juli 1979

Chockstart av Göteborgs FF räckte inte mot Leicester City

GÖTEBORG: Som väntat vann Leicester City en klar seger över Göteborgs FF, 4—1, men det var GFF som chockstartade med att göra ledningsmålet.

GFF visade prov på en hel del i matchen mot Leicester — men respekt det visade man aldrig för de engelska ligaproffsen. GFF lyckades hålla spelet förvånansvärt väl uppe och gjorde till allas förvåning matchens första mål.

Det dröjde nästan en hel halvtimme innan det målet föll. Det var Hans Grey som fick bollen i en hög av spelare och klippte till med ett stenhårt högerskott. Leicesters målvakt Mark Wallington hade inte någon chans att ta den bollen. Men GSS:s glädje blev inte långvarig. Det dröjde bara tre minuter innan Martin Henderson satte kvällens elegantaste mål. Han mötte en hörna med en flygande nick som sattes i ena stolproten. Men Leicester började matchen med ett mycket högt tempo och GSS försökte hänga med, även om de hade stora svårigheter i början. I matchens inledning utmärkte sig särskilt Leicesters förste målskytt Martin Henderson som är snabb och var ett verkligt mäktigt stopp.

Annars saknades den rätta skärpan i Leicesters matchenledning.

GFF spelade friskt däremot och var totalt respektlösa. Kid Lith försökte trycka sig fram på vänsterkanten, även om han för det mesta blev stoppad av Leicesters försvar. Lasse Carlsson gjorde likadant på högerkanten och bakom dem fanns Erling Öström som var en mycket duktig spelarfördelare.

Strax före första halvlekens slut gjorde så Leicester ett ledningsmål. Då en Leicester-spelare vände sig om på en femöring och klippte in ett stenhårt skott. Men fram till dess hade det gått förvånansvärt trögt för Leicester och man tappade stundtals humöret i båda lagen.

Efter 20 minuter av andra lek, visade Leicesters sin ö- na styrka. 1—3 gjorde John O'nick efter inlägg av Patrine. Burne som strax efter 1—4 på långskott. Sedan lång uppvisning av de proffsen.

● Martin Henderson i Leicester slänger sig fram och nickar in kvitteringsmålet mot GFF.

● GFF-försvaret kämpade väl mot de engelska vänen om det inte alltid var helt justa metoder..

Blåvitts Slocknade Stjärnor lyser ännu!

Av STEFAN LILJEHOLM

GÖTEBORG: I skuggan av de Stora Stjärnorna i Leicester spelade de Slocknande Stjärnorna i Blåvitt en mycket underhållande match mot GFF på Majvallen på tisdagseftermiddagen.

På planen fanns gamla storheter som "Bebban" Johansson och ter vardera i ett sådant förhållandevis högt tempo? frågade Arbe-

It is essential that you take plenty of photos on your pre-season tour... especially of our players looking slightly embarrassed at their humble surroundings A) City's exciting new signing Gregor Stevens... it's a ball Gregor. B) The splendid new Umbro strip gets its first airing. C) A Henderson header at the houses end. D) Mark Wallington makes a good save in front of a packed rockery.

A.

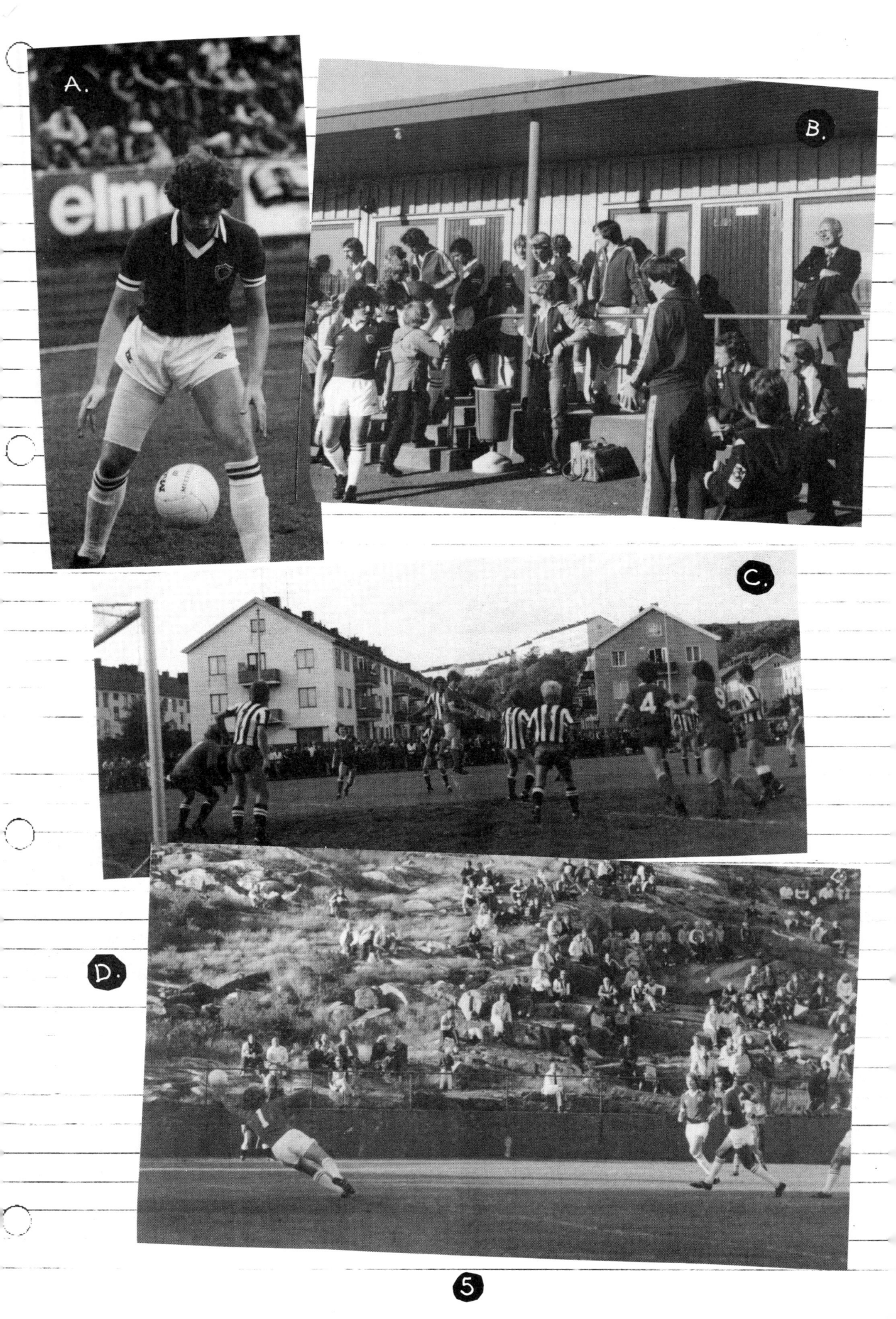

B.

C.

D.

❺

Haarlem Globetrotters

A year later Sue went on the pre-season tour of Holland and Germany as City prepared themselves for the rigours of the top flight...
A) Old habits die hard for this German guard. B) LCFC take the scoreboard at Haarlem.
C) Posing with Jock Wallace outside the 'supporters home'. D) Leicester pack the away end.

A Breath of Fresh Eire

The 1991-92 season may have ended beneath the Twin Towers of Wembley, but it began in front of "massed sheep on the bank behind the goal" according to Farley Pig who followed City on their pre-season tour of Ireland, taking in Monaghan, Shelbourne and Athlone.

A) Reid & Wright thrill the locals. B) Tony James in front of the Weed Bank. C) Ashley Ward. Would you pay £4M for a player that runs like a *girl*? D) We were going to mock this 'bus shelter' before we realised that it is three feet taller than our East Stand.

The Rodney Fern Gallery

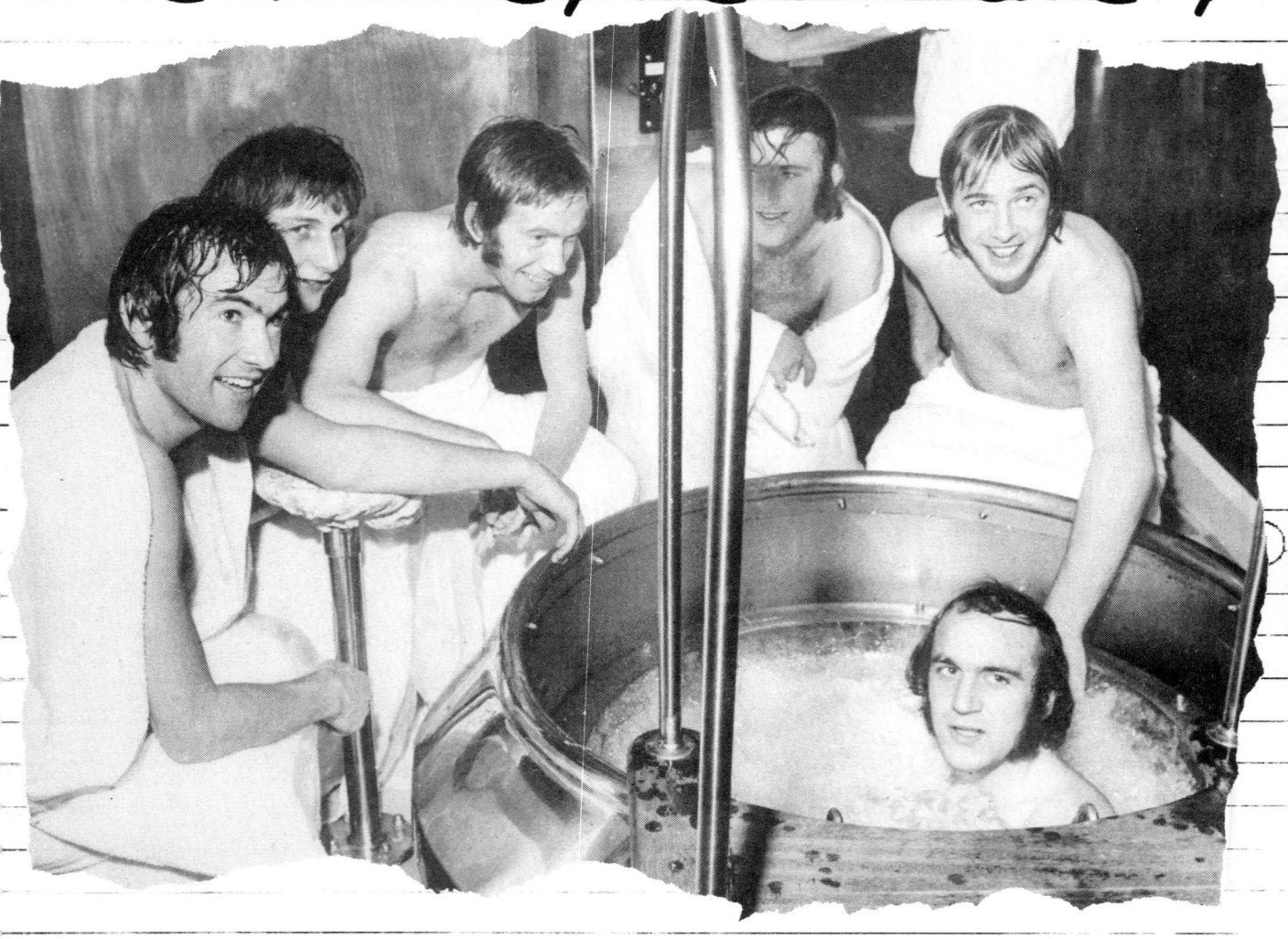

Rodney was a late sixties/early seventies Kop favourite with thinning pate and an eye for goal. Here's a photo (above) from September 1973 featuring City Greats (ish) Jon Sammels, Malcolm Munro, Steve Whitworth, Malcolm Partridge and The Birch boiling the mud off Rodney Fern's legs to make next weekend's half-time Bovril for the Pop Side...

Richard West of Newtown Linford sent in these two corking snaps (below) of:
"Rodney Fern trying to escape from my Uncle after an FA Cup tie at Rotherham in 1968".

Nectar of the Gods

Never mind yer Fox Fast Food... here are a couple of real slow burners donated to the Big Blue Scrapbook by Simon Kimber.

The City Ale was produced to celebrate our promotion to the (proper) First Division in 1983. Simon is sort of waiting for a big enough occasion to crack it open and unleash the sweet taste of success. Wembley Play Off Final victories and the lifting of the League Cup weren't deemed *quite* big enough. If I were you Simon, I would open it the next time we win so much as a corner... I've just given it a good shake and after sixteen years it looks a bit on the flat side...

On the other hand the stick of 'Leicester City' rock, made by *Rock Candy Kingdom*, looks as good and tasty as the day it was bought, four years ago, on Skeggy seafront.

Both together they would make a meal fit for a King (as long as the King didn't mind suffering a severe bout of botulism).

Colour Me Bad

Selected pages from my 'Caversham Football Colouring Book'. Not too good, I admit, even for a seven year old. I just can't understand it, I followed the instructions and everything...

On the following pages you should choose two teams to take part in a football match and colour a scene from the game. Use the details of colours found in this book. Perhaps you would like to write your own report of the game alongside the picture.

Manchester City v Leicester
— Colin Bell
— Peter Shilton

Leicester v Liverpool 3-2
— Keith Weller
— Emlen Huges

Leicester City F.C. v Leeds UTD F.C.

Leicester v Newcastle 1-0

New Fangled Changes

This is the sort of stuff that was falling out of programmes and onto the terraces back in 1971, but Ian Davidson picked it back up, kept it for twenty eight years and then sent it in to the Big Blue Scrapbook. It was all to do with the introduction of that new Toytown money with those fiddly new halfpennies that got wedged in the corner of your wallet.

Anyway, whoever designed this rather bossy leaflet obviously didn't have any 'Football Supporter' rub down letraset characters to hand. So we are represented by this orderly series of well dressed catalogue types who look as though they bought their tweed sports car jackets, bri-nylon blousons and fashionably narrow slacks from Fenwicks, or maybe Irish Menswear on the Clocktower (when it was class, mind). In fact the only queuers lowering the tone in any way are the whippersnappers on the left weighing up the chances of saving three bob by sneaking under the turnstile; and the raffish cad in the houndstooth golf trews 'watering his horse' in the Wing Stand entrance. Cheeky Blighter.

PRESENTED BY LEICESTER CITY FOOTBALL CLUB

THE MAN INSIDE SAYS

"BEFORE YE ENTER THESE GATES"

EXACT MONEY READY PLEASE

'THINK DECIMAL'

GROUND 30p (CHILDREN 15p) — ENCLOSURE 35p (CHILDREN 20p) — DOUBLE DECKER 50p — WING STAND 70p — MAIN STAND 80p

ADMISSION CHARGES REMAIN THE SAME

CONVERSION GUIDE....

NEW	£1	50p	10p	5p	2½p	2p	1p	½p
OLD	£1	10/-	2/-	1/-	6d	ABOUT 5d	OVER 2d	OVER 1d

Filbo Greetings

"Happy Birthday to Yooouuu!" Well, it will be if you are the lucky recipient of this rare 'Birthday Greetings Brother' card (left) featuring Joe Waters playing in the 1974 FA Cup Semi Final against Liverpool at Old Trafford. Despite receiving something in the region of 10,000 football related birthday cards in my life not one of them ever had Leicester City on it...

Paul Henderson sent the Jock Wallace Christmas card (below) in to the Big Blue Scrapbook with the message:

"You must let me have the card back in time for Chrimbo. It was given away with the programme in 1980 and things just wouldn't be the same without Jock's card. Every year I put it up on my mantlepiece to bring me festive fortune and a big yuletide stockingful of memories: Alan Young, Bobby Smith... Martin Henderson? Merry Christmas!"

These were simple times for the Filbo Christmas card... the nineties were to get much more complicated.

A) Christmas 1994... As soon as had Russ Carvell had applied the last brushstroke to this seasonal team group for the club's official Christmas card then Brian Little buggered off to Villa. Filbert the Fox was a late substitution with his head being stuck on top of 'Santa' Brian's.

B) Christmas 1995... A year later Russ took a couple of steps back to admire his completed masterpiece when the phone rang again. Mark McGhee had hightailed it to Wolves, and this time it was Steve Walsh who had to be papered over the gap.

C) Christmas 1996... Fortunately no hat trick for Russ and we all 'Have an Ice Christmas' as Martin O'Neill stays put.

A.

B.

C.

Cheer Up Mark McGhee

Now, the last thing we want to do is further demonise Mark McGhee, BUT, here are two photos of him supposedly playing in a 'charity' match on Cosby park. A) shows him drawing a moustache on a photo of the luvverly Queen Mother (booooo!) and B) shows him attempting to kidnap Neil, John and Mark, Simon Kimber's god children, while no one's looking. What a rotter!

Above right is an article from the *Daily Mail* sent in by Tim Burke, explaining that we were right and he was wrong all along..... while below right is the postcard that some genius thought of distributing among City fans in Madrid before the Atletico UEFA Cup game. Thanks again Mark, you helped City get where they are today (by leaving).

Daily Mail, Tuesday, January 19, 1999 — Page 69

SOCCER EXCLUSIVE: Mark McGhee, the man the fans love to hate

I knew I'd pay for letting Leicester down...maybe the price was too high

Soccer outcast: McGhee became a pariah

HUGH JAMIESON finds the sacked Wolves boss eager to resurrect his ailing career even if he is forced to go abroad

THERE was a time, not so long ago, when Mark McGhee was widely considered the brightest young managerial prospect in Britain.

Top clubs queued up for the services of the dapper, smooth-talking Scot who counted the likes of Manchester United's Alex Ferguson among his friends, confidants and most ardent admirers.

Yet, rather than climb an inviting ladder to success, McGhee has found himself stumbling from rung to rung, collecting more cuffs around the ear than pats on the back from the public he was so anxious to please.

Instead of being lauded as a soccer saint, he found himself branded a Judas at Reading and Leicester. And he was labelled an arrogant failure by fans of Wolves, whose Premiership dreams he manifestly failed to fulfil.

McGhee now lives in splendid isolation as befits a man regarded by many as a soccer pariah. He agonises over where it all went wrong and contemplates how to kick-start his shattered career.

Doors in this country, which once opened for him to slip in and out of with an alacrity that raised such sceptical eyebrows, may now be closed. McGhee seems to sense it himself. In an exclusive interview with *Sportsmail* he revealed: 'The day after losing my job at Wolves I began a language course in Spanish. It's not that I thought my next job would be in Spain but because I didn't have any fear about learning languages or going abroad.

'Naturally, I would like another job in England but if that doesn't happen it wouldn't worry me moving abroad. I played in Germany for a couple of years, enjoyed the experience and speak the language.

'It might be that I have to start afresh abroad, achieve the right kind of success and provide the

'Languages may land me a job'

opportunity to build a bridge back to England and re-establish myself.'

It has been two months since McGhee's Molineux reign was suddenly and dramatically brought to an end because he was unable to produce a Wolves team which offered a realistic hope of promotion from the First Division.

No tears were shed at his departure. On the contrary, his demise produced smirks among supporters at Leicester and Reading and suggestions that he got what he deserved. McGhee is no mug. He knows the score. 'I can understand the Reading and Leicester fans now laughing up their sleeves about my sacking at Wolves.

'I don't feel resentment towards them because that's the way it goes sometimes in this game and you've got to be big enough to take it.'

He thinks he is big enough and is prepared to devour a large slice of humble pie.

But at the same time the man who enjoyed a hugely successful playing career in Scotland and further afield is determined to set the record straight, as he sees it, concerning his controversial moves from Reading and Leicester.

McGhee can cope with being despised in some quarters, but not others. He said: 'I felt entitled to leave Reading because I'd done a very good job there and had been given permission to go by the chairman.

'I don't think that the fans had any right to feel aggrieved, but Leicester was different because I knew I would be letting people down and there was going to be a price to pay.

'I realised I would leave myself open to ridicule. I had to take Wolves into the Premiership, that was my brief — but it didn't happen. Looking back, in terms of my reputation and how people perceived me afterwards, the price was probably too high.

'I felt people at Wolves had a picture of me that really wasn't true. They felt I was mercenary to the point of being arrogant and egotistical - someone who could walk out on Leicester to join Wolves just because it suited me.

'What they didn't realise was that it was an agonising decision for me

'Leaving Leicester was agonising'

to take because I'd had such a fantastic working relationship with Martin George, then Leicester chairman. It took a lot of influence from people around me to persuade me that the move to Wolves was the right thing to do.

'People thought I made the decision in total isolation and simply said "I'm off". But it wasn't like that at all.'

McGhee agreed that his image had been sullied — and it became worse. He added: 'The way I was portrayed at Wolves, especially in the media, is something which has haunted me. I was totally bamboozled by things I was supposed to have said about other clubs and teams. I was either misquoted or my words were corrupted — and this led to the idea that I was someone prepared to shout my mouth off about anything and everything.'

Whether or not he was given a raw deal, 41-year-old McGhee has a major restoration job on his hands and he is adamant that he will face it head on.

He said: 'I am determined to show people the real Mark McGhee. I have been doing a lot of thinking and self-analysing since I left Wolves to work out where I go from here.

'I haven't lost my self-belief — but you can bet that I will most certainly be a different person next time out after a chastening experience like this one.

'It will be no good turning up for a job interview and telling them I'm Mark McGhee and have managed Reading, Leicester and Wolves so they must give me the job.

'It's going to be about convincing people I've got fresh ideas, that I know how I want my team to play — and that I still want to be a top manager.'

Worthy sentiments — but whether McGhee will be delivering his job application in English, German or Spanish remains to be seen.

ARE YOU WATCHING MARK McGHEE?

ATHLETICO MADRID vs THE BLUE ARMY

While City take on Athletico Madrid, in the cut and thrust of European football, Wolves will be travelling to the Mighty Fulham!! Please take this opportunity to remember old friends who've fallen on hard times.

_____
_____
_____
_____
_____

Signed _____

'This is meant as a humourous and goodhearted gloat!! Please **DO NOT** use foul and abusive language - it's just not necessary!!

STAMP

MARK McGHEE

Manager
Woverhampton Wanderers FC
Molineux Stadium
Waterloo Road
Wolverhampton
WV1 4QR

The Helen Hyatt

When we featured Helen's early-eighties snaps from the tunnel region in The FOX (see below) we concentrated on the close-up, left ear'ole comings and goings from the confines of the white-washed tunnel. A dramatically involved and claustrophobic series in itself, but Helen was also known to point her lens in the direction of the pitch and, in the event of promotion, even behind her into the Main Stand. At the end of the 1982-83 season a 0-0 draw with Burnley appeared to have clinched promotion for City.. A) Shows Kevin MacDonald, Gordon Milne, John O'Neill, Gerry Daly and Gary Lineker in a scaredy, panicky headlong rush for the tunnel before they are enveloped by a crowd invasion of floppy fringes, Pringle jumpers and the odd left-over skinhead. Photo B) The Peelers struggle to hold back the seething masses, many of them in burgundy tank tops and grey slip-ons (probably). Photo C) Look carefully and you can see some City heroes celebrating promotion... look there, behind Tommy English.
Then we got home to find out a League Inquiry had been ordered after a pitch invasion at Derby. Damn those Sheepshaggers!

Here's a confused Alan Smith thinking, "Bloimey, there's some bird dangling roight down in the tunnel, loik."

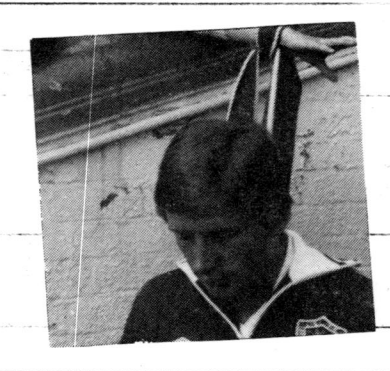

Gerry Daly being hung from the tunnel spikes by one particularly exacting fan's City scarf. Generally it's considered more 'traditional' to at least wait for kick-off before starting to gripe at the lads, even then stopping short of murder

The Boy Lineker, aged seven

An insufficiently dangling Helen's-eye-view of Jim Melrose, get yer abseiling krampons out next week, me duck.

That's more like it! It's Kevin MacDonald treating himself to a fruitful snotty.

Tunnel-based plodder about to be enveloped by the monstrous, terrifying shadow of Kevin Keegan's Bubble perm

Tunnel Collection

A.

B.

C.

The Geoff Scott's Aunty's rubbish tip photo collection

Geoff Scott was a blond, gangly left-back/centre-half who turned out for City from 1980 to 1982... his main claim to fame would be playing in the side that clinched the Second Division Championship with a 1-0 win at Orient. Anyway, me and my best mate Jon (proud of his 'Sammels' spelling incidentally) were grubbing around amongst the litter in the abandoned quarry field between Huncote and Croft when we happened upon priceless treasure. And I don't mean a copy of 'Whitehouse' (in fact that may have been the one time when we didn't find any weathered, scrunched up porn). No this was, arguably, even better. Geoff Scott, who was believed to live in the region of Stoney Stanton, appeared to have accidentally left some rubbish behind in a big pile in the gateway of the quarry field. There was an unpaid telephone bill from when he lived in Stoke, and some photos of him taken at the Orient game. I can only assume that the photographer was his auntie, or some other middle-aged female admirer because

Cough up £40.98 Geoff, or else Post Office Telecommunications will get you...

A.

B.

she appears in several of the photos. How kind of Geoff to throw them away less than a year later. Anyhow... Geoff's loss is our gain and this look at City's great day in East London, with a definite Geoff Scott bias, goes as follows...

A) Our intrepid duo getting off the bus...
B) "We didn't see many of the London sights where we went, but we did see this police dog sitting near a keep left sign."
C) A full City end and some pre-match tension.
D) Oh look there's Geoff, "Coooo-eeeee, GEOFF!"
E) "Come over Geoff, I want a photo ..."
F) "Here's one of us during the pitch invasion..."
"Oooh Mam, should they be doing that?"
G) "Oooh dear... they've broken it now. I think we'd better go, before that police dog comes."

Ill Advised David Pleat Photos

A pair of back page snaps of David Pleat that probably wouldn't have been taken if he'd thought twice about them. The wheelbarrow shot suggests that his new £250,000 signing Wayne Clarke is rubbish which, of course, he was... the one with the luvverly ladies should produce a dirty laugh for anyone who read the Sun in 1987 and knows the gritty details of why Tottenham sacked him. Phew!

My crap Union Jack flag

This flag was waved about by me at the front of the Kop for much of the diabolically bad 1977-78 relegation season. Armstrong, Davies, Webb, Waddle, White..... never can so many has-beens, never-were's and plainly no good players have been celebrated on one, hanky sized Union Jack.

Read All Abaaaaaadit

MONDAY

RAMS SAVAGED BY FOXES: REPORT, PICTURES

Telegraph

Jurgen from Belper in Derbyshire stole this super momento of City's 4-0 thrashing of Derby in 1998 from outside his local newsagents and insisted that we stick it in the Big Blue Scrapbook... A nice reminder of the day we knocked the pride out of Pride Park.

Scott Caricatures in the Sunday Extra

When the old 'Buff' Saturday evening Sports Mercury folded in September 1979, we were offered the disappointing alternative of the 'Sunday Extra'... a thin, sorry, white Mercury publication given away free with your national Sunday Paper. It was rubbish. No longer could we gather round the newsagents door on a Saturday evening with the other regular Buff readers, waiting for the Mercury van to drop off its precious cargo of hastily assembled results and league tables with a thump onto the pavement. The only good-ish things in the Sunday Extra, were these 'Scott' cartoons, which I painstakingly cut out every week, coloured in, and stuck on a home made poster...

Caricatures shown: Lineker, Young, Kelly, Smith, Rofe, Buchanan — all signed "Scott"

SUNDAY EXTRA — Leicestershire's own Sunday paper

Dave Goodacre's miracle sticker

Foxile Dave Goodacre, who started watching City in 1954, runs the 'Wishing Well' pub in Heywood, Lancs, a favoured watering hole (every pun intended) of City fans stopping en route to Blackburn or Bolton.

One Monday early in 1998, after City had beaten Leeds 1-0, Dave discovered this Martin O'Neill sticker that had appeared stuck to a first storey window of the pub. None of his regulars knew who had stuck it there, so dismissing such far-fetched theories as drunken locals messing about after hours, Dave prefers to believe that this was a genuine miracle.

Dave is a firm believer in miracles ever since City beat Liverpool, Manchester United and Coventry away all in the same season.

Sweat Banned

What Keith Weller, Jeff Blockley and Dennis Rofe wear today, the eleven year old boys of Brockington College will surely wear tomorrow.
Except with the designer twist that we wore them *under our watches*.
Where, to be honest, they seemed to create more sweat than they ever absorbed.

Mick's Nicked Madrid Poster

"We spotted them on a billboard in the early hours of the morning as we wandered around the ground", explains Mick Iwaszko. "We thought they would make good souvenirs of our first trip abroad following City. It might be another thirty five years before we qualify again. We carefully removed them and then legged it back to our hotel. Back home the following day my poster was still in fairly good nick so I made a picture frame for it and it takes pride of place at the top of the stairs. Despite the fact that there are only two of them in this country my daughter doesn't look too impressed with it, or the five sizes too big t-shirt that I bought her."

INGLATERRA El rival del Atlético en UEFA ganó y ya es tercero de la Premier League

Leicester, ¡qué miedo!

(translation: "Leicester, How Scary." Were they being sarky?)

Sew on patches and so on...

In the olden days you couldn't just walk down to Fox Leisure and pick your replica shirt off the peg and bung a £50 note over the counter. No. You had to get your Granny to knit you a City shirt, and then you had to buy a badge separate to sew onto it. And it looked rubbish.

In the seventies one of the many trends that crossed the Atlantic was that of the sew on patch, which not only covered a hole in the knee of your jeans or the back of your denim jacket, but could also make a bold statement. Like 'Make Love, Not War' or 'Up Leicester!'. Grateful thanks go to Sue Williamson whose patch collection is sewn into the Big Blue Scrapbook below...

Bored of Directors

Here are two articles from the Sunday Express and Shoot! which thoroughly endorse the traditional view that City's directors have always been tighter than a camel's arse in a sandstorm. Jimmy Bloomfield's heart-felt outpouring leaves us to think what might have been, while James Mossop tries manfully to paint a bright face on the terrible situation that City were in early in the 1983-84 season. Thankfully his hunch that we would eventually stay up proved correct.

Gordon does not despair over lowly Leicester

by JAMES MOSSOP

AMONG THE decorative trophies and priceless souvenirs gathered by Leicester City in the days when their fame travelled the world ahead of them stands a reminder of their plight in 1983.

There, above the cocktail bar in the corner of the large panelled boardroom where directors used to entertain their guests, sits a price list.

Everyone pays for his drinks these days. With debts rising beyond £1 million and Leicester tipped the length and breadth of the country for relegation to the Second Division, scope for generosity is extremely limited.

They are top people fallen on hard times. Their home in Filbert Street is one of the best. Colourfully painted seats fill the stands. The corridors and dressing-rooms gleam. Everything about the place is big.

Problem

But in that boardroom, with its deep blue carpet, high ceiling and mounted elephant tusks from the Transvaal, there has been only one win to talk about since Leicester rose proudly from the Second Division last May.

Around 11,000 a match have been watching this season's honest toil. They need 15,000 to break even. Their problem is typical of that facing football below the very top of the First Division.

Trying to nudge Leicester into a proper direction is Gordon Milne, the 45-year-old manager who followed Bill Shankly and Tommy Docherty into the No. 4 shirt at Preston and has since become a master at the art of survival.

For nine years as manager of Coventry, after a carefree playing career spent mostly in the legendary Liverpool side of the 'sixties, he kept Lady Godiva's team in the First Division while bigger names such as Spurs and Manchester United were dropping out for spells in the Second.

Coventry existed on small gates, big hearts and the development of youngsters, seven of whom—Les Sealey, Danny Thomas, Gary Gillespie, Paul Dyson, Mark Hateley, Garry Thompson and Steve Whitton—were sold for £3m in the summer to buy something close to solvency.

Powerful

Now Milne, 15 months into his contract at Leicester, has to keep his team of novices in the top flight and develop the club while he looks up from the bottom of the table saying : "I cannot spend a penny on new players."

As he spoke his powerful centre-half, Bob Hazell, an aggressive giant who has inspired a remarkable improvement in the young player alongside him, David Rennie, was being treated for an injury that will keep him out for another three weeks.

There is no obvious replacement on the staff and the constant engagement of Milne's telephone line means he is trying to borrow a defender. He could not afford the £900-a-week and £150-a-point requirements of Liverpool's Phil Thompson. Such is life when you are in trouble.

But there is a surprising optimism in Milne's voice when he says : "At this time of year when I was at Liverpool we used to say, 'Right, here come the real footballing months — November, December, January, February.' These are the sorting out days.

"You have been through those early days of fast pitches, eager fresh players and wonder goals going in. This is when the season settles down.

"There is no pressure or despair here. I am confident we will be all right. When we achieved promotion I could see the problems that lay ahead. A lot of our players had very limited experience of the First Division.

"How would they handle it ? They are learning all the time. They are eager to learn. The spirit is the same as last season. There is laughter in the dressing-room.

"They realise they have to be craftier and sharper than

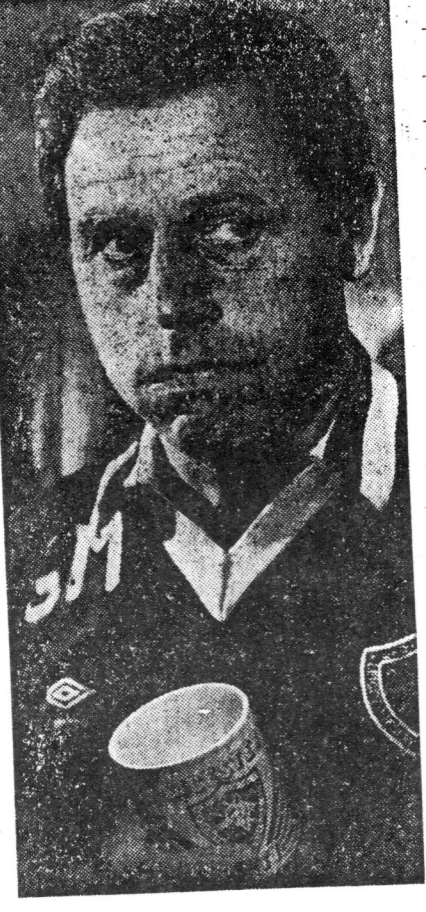

GORDON MILNE ... "football is such magic for me"

26

they were last season and they know our form has picked up over the last month.

"We don't over-coach them. We don't have too many meetings. Most of my meetings are with the bank manager. Board meetings are usually about one thing. Money.

"The public are being patient. They know our problems. But I would rather be getting stick at the bottom of the First Division than slaps on the back at the top of the Second."

Milne has lived with the harsh reaction of some supporters. When he was at Coventry, working that miracle of survival, he received threatening telephone calls.

He was hit by a tomato, an irate group hurled their season tickets at him and others pushed letters through his car windows.

Enough, you would think, to make anyone get out of the precarious business of football management.

"That never crosses my mind," he says. "I went to watch Birmingham the other night and as a neutral I always find myself looking at the crowd. They were all there, living in hope for their team, and proudly wearing their scarves—blokes with probably not much money who had taken their kids along.

"I go and watch the youngsters play on a Sunday morning and it is all this, the playing and watching, that makes football such magic for me. I love it.

"That is why it is hard to tell a youngster he is not going to make the grade. But I always point out people like Alan Devonshire, Cyrille Regis and Graham Roberts who were lost to professional clubs as youngsters but were picked up later in non-League football and have since played for England.

Changing

"I think football is changing for the better. It will never die. Clubs are realising they can no longer pay out what isn't coming in.

"We are not even holding our own financially at the moment but we are working on it. If small businesses were run along the lines of some football clubs there would not be enough money left to feed the wife and kids.

"It is a pity about the financial mess because there is a great spirit within the game. This was evident recently when we played Southampton and the heaviest rain I have ever seen flooded the pitch.

"It became impossible. The ball was stopping dead and at one point Steve Lynex went down and thrashed about breast-stroke fashion. But both teams were trying to play. No one complained or queried the conditions with the referee, who in the end had no option but to abandon it."

Milne reckoned Leicester would have won that match and taken three valuable points. But as he looks at the long, uphill haul, he says: "I sleep easy because I know that everything about the place is honest and healthy. You only toss and turn when you know things are sour."

This time last year Leicester were 15th in the Second Division. Milne slept soundly and Leicester were promoted. A year on they are poor, honest and beleaguered at the wrong end of Division One.

But I am backing them to stay up.

LEICESTER City fans get a chance to indulge in a brief spell of nostalgia this Saturday when Orient visit Filbert Street.

The return of Orient manager Jimmy Bloomfield to the club where he was in charge for six years, will bring back memories of the success times Leicester enjoyed under him.

Seventh place in the First Division and a run to the Semi-Final of the F.A. Cup — both happened during Bloomfield's reign at Filbert Street. And, with Leicester now languishing in the Second Division, it is a worthy thought that Bloomfield — and the First Division good time days — might still be there but for a disagreement which mushroomed out of control.

Bloomfield says: "I left on a matter of principle. I was happy there for five of my six years but the person behind my departure is no longer with the club. I have no bad feelings whatsoever towards the club — it's a smashing place with wonderful people.

'LEICESTER COULD HAVE BEEN ANOTHER LIVERPOOL'

JIMMY BLOOMFIELD (Orient)

"But I think they thought it cost them a million pounds when I left. I was as sad as anyone to see the club slide from tenth in the First Division the season I left, to just missing relegation from Division Two."

Bloomfield reveals that a director's refusal to allow him to buy winger Peter Taylor, then with Crystal Palace, probably cost Leicester a major trophy at that time. "Taylor would have given us the perfect side," he said. "I wanted him to finish off everything I'd been working for.

"But one director wouldn't agree and we lost him to Spurs. I believe he would have made all the difference and would probably have been the final push towards landing a trophy.

"We were always one player short that year. But despite that, when we played Liverpool, we would have gone top of the First Division for the first time in 25 years, had we won. That showed how close we were to success.

"That side that also reached the Cup Semi-Final was a great one. Shilton, Whitworth, Rofe, Blockley, Sims, Weller, Sammels, Kember, Birchenall, Earle, Worthington, Garland. At the time, people told me they were playing the best football any Leicester side had produced for 25 years.

"I still believe that Peter Shilton was a better goalkeeper then than he has been at any stage since. I'll never change my opinion on that. And some of the football we played was absolutely fantastic; some of the best of the time from any side.

"It disappointed me to see Leicester go down. So much work had been done at the club in my time by so many people. Relegation was a poor reward. I had the feeling when we were going so well that if we'd got the crowds we would have become another Liverpool. But the lack of support held us back."

Franky Wortho is the

Soon after Frank was criminally allowed to leave Filbert Street for Bolton Wanderers, he was given star billing in the *Daily Mirror's* outrageous lid-lifting sex series 'The Love Game'.... phew what a scorcher!
Below are photos of Franky before, during and after official Sex God status.

FIVE NIGHTS A WEEK (but never on Friday) FRANK

Reporters: JOHN JACKSON and JILL PALMER
Photographer: KENT GAVIN

IT'S Saturday afternoon again, and out on the football field, Frank Worthington is doing what he likes best.

Twenty thousand pairs of eyes watch him move with the elegance and speed that have always made him something special among a very special set.

Frank Worthington is playing soccer. He has played in front of more people—100,000 when he turned out for England. And probably he has also played better in his time. One day, sooner rather than later, Frank Worthington has to stop running.

At twenty-nine, playing for Bolton Wanderers, he knows that his golden days in this country have gone. He will almost certainly never play for England again.

And amid the sweat of Second Division football, the nagging thoughts are always there now: Could Frank Worthington really have done better? Probably he could. In that case, why didn't he?

SATURDAY night is here again ... and Frank Worthington is doing what he likes second best.

This time perhaps a dozen pairs of eyes are watching him as he toys with a drink in a club. They watch him with the same eagerness that the boys and their fathers showed that afternoon ... Only these eyes don't notice the magic in his boots.

They see the blond streaks in his hair, the tall, lean body, the expensive jeans and coat, and the Elvis Presley badge stuck rakishly in his lapel.

These are girls' eyes drinking in the flamboyant Soccer extrovert who attracts women like a Cup Final attracts crowds, who outrages the game's establishment ... and who basks in every minute of the reflected notoriety.

Frank by name and frank by nature, he talks openly a few hours later about his life. And he reveals that from the moment he played his first game as a professional footballer he realised there was as much fun to be had OFF the field as on it.

Worthington confesses: "My bed wasn't for sleeping, it was simply for birding. I was at it five nights a week, with rarely the same woman twice and often the odd quick one before a match."

Saturday night has always been the night for sex after Soccer. He says: "That's the unwinding time.

"A player who has been all keyed up for a match must unwind after the final whistle blows. And how better than with a few jars and then into bed with a girl—or two."

All of which neatly encapsulates the Frank Worthington philosophy of loving his job — and loving his loving.

"Sometimes my life's been so full that it's overflowed, leaving me physically and emotionally exhausted," he says. "But if I should drop down dead this minute no one could say I haven't squeezed the maximum from my life.

"I've got no regrets about anything. After all, we're only on this Earth for a visit."

There was one period when Frank Worthington's life-style caught up with him with a vengeance. It happened in 1972 while he was with his first club Huddersfield Town. Liverpool made a £150,000 offer for him ... but the deal fell through after he failed his medical check because of high blood pressure.

The doctor who examined him warned that he was using up too much of his energy off the field.

"That was a shattering experi-

Tomorrow: The Be

28

One True God of Love

DAILY MIRROR, Tuesday, February 7, 1978   PAGE 15

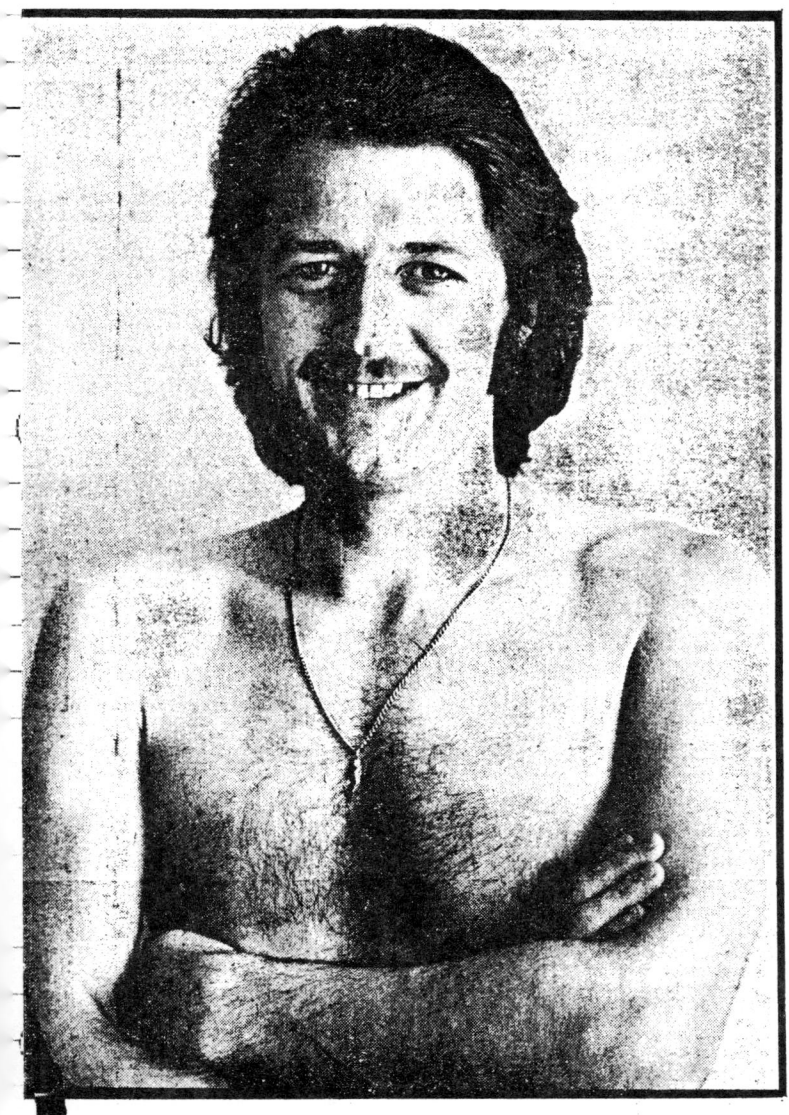

Football killed my marriage

WILD-LIVING Frank Worthington is today surveying the ruins of his marriage to Swedish blonde Birgitta Egermalm.

As the Mirror revealed exclusively yesterday, the couple have finally ended their stormy relationship.

Birgitta knew nothing of football and its stars the day she met Frank seven years ago when he was on a holiday jaunt to Majorca with his pal George Best.

But she knows all about the game now. And she says bitterly: "Football killed our marriage. Frank lived only for football — and for himself."

When her romance with Worthington began, he was playing for Huddersfield Town and emerging as one of the brightest hopes on the soccer scene.

Birgitta was one of the few girls he had ever met who had never heard of him.

Yet they were instantly attracted to each other, and a few months later she travelled to England to spend a month with him.

They married in 1973 and now have two children—Frank Junior, who was born a few months before the wedding, and a three-year-old daughter, Kim.

But there was trouble almost from the start—much of it to do with Frank's lifestyle. Birgitta frequently stormed off back to Sweden, and Frank also walked out.

Birgitta says: "When I married I had no idea of the life of a footballer, I didn't even know who George Best was.

"It is always difficult in any case for a marriage to survive when the husband and wife come from different countries.

"But Frank made me depressed so many times because of his wanderings."

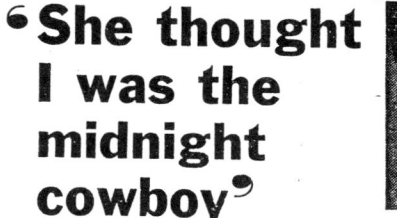

BIRGITTA: Unhappy

'She thought I was the midnight cowboy'

A WHOLE galaxy of girls have shared Frank Worthington's bed. But none compares with the showbiz groupie he describes as "the most amazing bird I've ever had."

They met in a nightclub when he was wearing a brown skin jacket with leather fringes.

He says: "I was standing on my own when this girl walked up and said, 'I've got to talk to you. I've seen you around and I fancy you rotten.'

"She said I was the Midnight Cowboy, and nothing I told her would change her mind."

The girl insisted on calling him Joe—after Joe Buck, the handsome stud played by John Voight in the Hollywood movie.

"It was like that all the time," says Worthington. "But what a night, what an experience. She's the best woman I've ever taken to bed.

"If they were all like her I'd willingly swap my football boots for a horse and spurs."

He also looks back fondly on the beautiful blonde he calls The Lady in the Shower.

He eyed her up in a hotel restaurant, and when he rang her room she said: "I'll be down after my shower."

She reappeared wearing a sexy dress ... with nothing underneath.

Worthington discovered her secret when they went to her room.

"She was magic," he says. "It was great."

VOIGHT: Cowboy

WORTHINGTON: "For me it was look at 'em, love 'em and leave 'em. I never really minded who it was."

ence," he says. And, pointing to the ceiling: "For me it was a sign from Him upstairs that I'd better start scoring on Saturday afternoons instead of five nights a week in bed.

"My stamina was just being sapped. The sun was always up before my nights ended."

Shortly after that he had a nervous breakdown. But eventually his health settled and he moved to Leicester City.

He lost his England place after being capped eight times. His next stop was Second Division Bolton.

Now he admits that the late nights and the eager womanising played a large part in what should have been a brilliant career.

THE arrogance and flamboyance of Frank Worthington were created from the humblest of beginnings.

He was born in the small Yorkshire village of Shelf, near Halifax, and followed his older brothers Bob and Dave into professional football.

Bob and Dave started off with Halifax Town, but Frank got a trial with Huddersfield and was promptly taken on. At twenty five he was leading the England attack.

Soon he had a Mustang car, went to top nightclubs, palled up with George Best ... it was fun all the way.

Worthington says: "I would dance the night away at discos. I never wanted to go home while everybody else was around having a ball.

"Often I'd take a girl back to my flat and she'd stay for a couple of days. Then she'd move on—to make way for another.

"I never really minded who it was. Sometimes, though, I'd wake up in the morning and look at the face next to me on the pillow and wonder what the hell I was up to."

He recalls the time a blonde chambermaid caught his eye while he was packing his bag after an overnight stay in an hotel.

The team coach was standing outside with its engine running, and the other players were in their seats.

He pulled the girl on to his bed, took off her black uniform ... and 'scored' again.

"It was a way of life. "Perhaps it didn't do my blood pressure any good, but it was great for my state of mind. And I don't regret one naked minute of it!" he says.

Like many footballers he always insisted that the loving had to stop on certain fixed days. "I gave myself Friday night off plus one other night," he says "I just had to allow myself some time for training with the lads."

Those lads knew him as Elvis —because he idolised the pop king. Recently he sent a wreath to the dead singer's home town to mark what would have been his birthday.

Life as one of Soccer's sex symbols has brought its share of tragedy to Frank Worthington. Today he stares at the ruins of his broken marriage.

A new chapter is opening in his personal life. Professionally he wistfully surveys the big-money scene across the Atlantic.

But the mood soon changes.

Suddenly jaunty again, he talks about the one big thrill he still wants to experience ... the Rio carnival in South America. "I've heard it's the greatest rave-up anywhere," he says.

And Frank Worthington wouldn't want to miss that.

THE LOVE GAME

st nights of my life

Er........Headlines

No one said it was easy summing up 90 minutes of thrilling, pulsating football in one snappy phrase with no long words in it... but sometimes you have to wonder how hard some sub editors are trying. During the 1980-81 season the Sunday Extra came up with a long string of lazy, punny, off the peg headlines to describe City's matches as they hurtled towards relegation...

'BE-'WICHED' (City lose to Ipswich); 'OUT-GUNNED' (City lose to Arsenal); 'SORE-THORNS' (City lose at the Hawthorns); 'WOLVES TAMED' (City beat Wolves); 'BLUNDERLAND' (City lose to Sunderland); 'DISUNITED' (City lose to Man United); 'CITY SPUR' (City beat Spurs). The only reason 'CITY HAMMERED' didn't appear was because West Ham weren't in the First Division...

BE-'WICHED!
OUT-GUNNED!
SORE—THORNS
WOLVES TAMED
BLUNDERLAND
DISUNITED
CITY SPUR

The best headlines during the Jock Wallace era always appeared in the *Sunday Express*, partly because they only featured us when we did something brilliant. They weren't particularly clever... just good and *punchy*.

THE WALLACE WHIZZ-KIDS TAKE CHARGE

City beat Orient 5-3...

The famous 'Keith Weller's White Tights' mauling of Norwich in the FA Cup...

Leicester leave them gasping
TEENAGERS TAKE NORWICH APART!

WALLACE'S KIDS ROCK CHAMPIONS

Two victories over Liverpool...

Fans on rampage as Leicester clinch title
WALLACE: WE HAVE NO FEARS

WALLACE'S WHIZZ-KIDS STUN KOP!

Championship Day at Orient...

....and a 2-1 win over Newcastle...steady on!

Wallace's whiz-kids serve up success for fickle fans
LEICESTER LEAP IN AS GOLDEN BABES SPARKLE

King of the Wing

'Lenny, Lenny Glover, Lenny Glover on the wi-ng. Lenny, Lenny Glover, Lenny Glover is our KING!' Such a legendary wing wizard as Len Glover was bound to come under intense media scrutiny... but this is going *too far*. Simon Smith ripped this photo out of his 'Bobby Charlton Annual' and sent it in to the Big Blue Scrapbook with the following observations:

"How's this for media intrusion, 1968 style? Who could have known that this was merely the thin end of the wedge, as far as the media interfering in football was concerned? One minute they're sticking a camera up your nose, as if it was an endoscope, the next they're telling you what time your games have to kick off."

But nothing, not even having his name spelt wrong on this cheapo football card, can make Lenny lose his cockerknee cool...

LEICESTER CITY CLOVER

Tears for Souvenirs

Big Blue Scrapbook curator Derek Hammond paid one quid for this kakky t-shirt because he bought it after the 1993 Play Off Final when we lost to Swindon. And it is so horrible, cheaply chucked together and tatty that he was still robbed. And what does this mysterious mantra mean? For the record it reads: "LEICESTER...XES FOXES FOXES FOXES FOXES FOXES FOXE LEICESTER LEICESTER FOXES FOXES LEICESTER LEICESTER." And that 'foxes' head is actually a wolf borrowed from the AS Roma badge. Look →

Mind you, what do you expect for a quid... a bleedin' Armani suit?

Possibly registering even higher on the tatty arsed foul cash in scale is this 'Wembley Play Off' scarf from the same year, sent in by Paul Henderson. "It really is horrible..." says Paul, "...and the fringing came away when we put it out of the car window.. There was a 100 mile long piece of yellow thread on the M1 that night, compounding our misery."

It might be a sad specimen but at least it features the traditional Leicester er...crown and crossed flags.

Tickets Please

You know when you are young and you like, tell a lie? Well I told my cousin, who was a Villa fan, that Filbert Street was better than Villa Park and that the map on the back of the ticket was a true representation of our ground. I don't see him anymore but I'd love to know how old he was when he realised the truth...

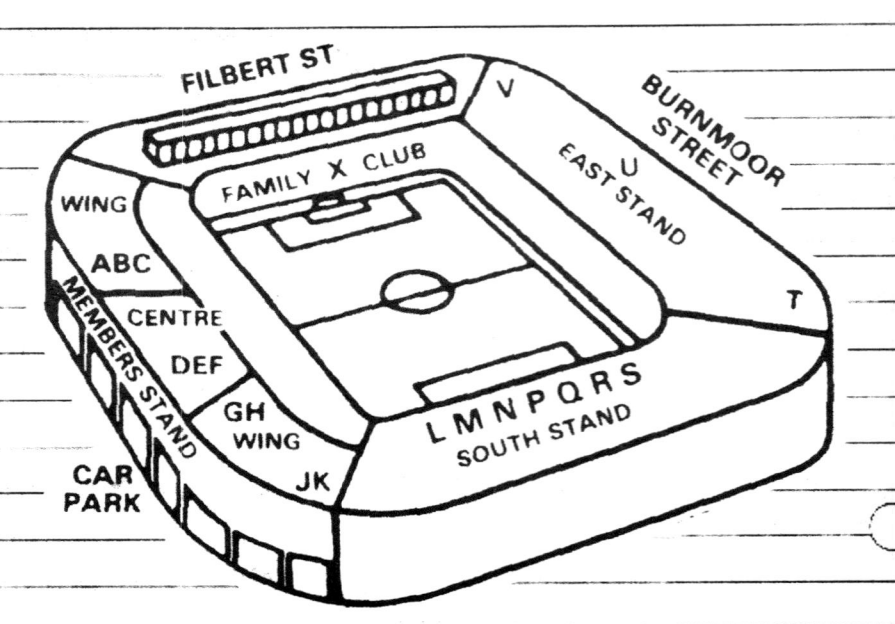

These two tickets, sent in by Clive Payne, are from consecutive seasons in the early seventies, but note the subtle differences.

In March 1971 you could pay 35p to stand anywhere in the Spion Kop which was known simply as 'Z', and you were advised to 'take up your position by 2.30pm.'

Only a year later the Kop had been penned off into four sections and the price had risen to 45p (a massive 28% increase) with punters now being advised to arrive ONE HOUR before kick off. Get stuffed! Mind you, 45p to see us beat Manchester United 2-0 has to be a bargain at any point in history.

The next two pages are strictly divided into Good & Bad tickets.... See if you can spot your own personal Best Day of Your Life/ Humiliating Nightmare match...

Good

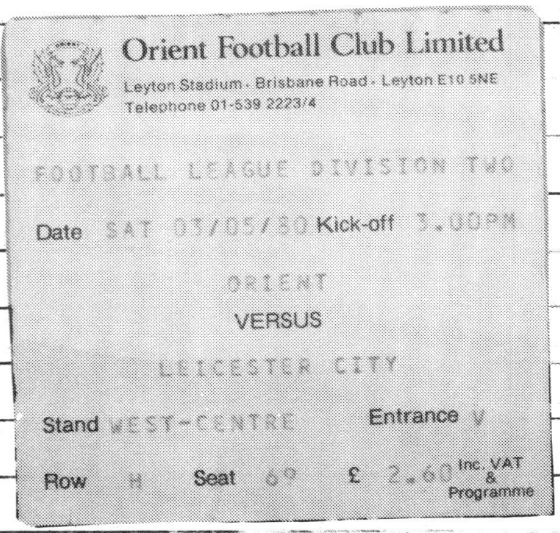

Orient Football Club Limited
Leyton Stadium · Brisbane Road · Leyton E10 5NE
Telephone 01-539 2223/4

FOOTBALL LEAGUE DIVISION TWO
Date SAT 05/05/90 Kick-off 3.00PM
ORIENT
VERSUS
LEICESTER CITY
Stand WEST-CENTRE   Entrance V
Row H   Seat 69   £2.60 Inc. VAT & Programme

Sheffield Wednesday FC
PLEASE TAKE UP YOUR SEAT 30 MINS. BEFORE KICK-OFF
COCA-COLA CUP FINAL REPLAY
LEICESTER CITY v MIDDLESBROUGH
WED 16 APR 1997 Kick Off 07:45 PM
SOUTH STAND ENTRANCE E
GANGWAY 16 ROW N SEAT 79 PRICE 32.00

Liverpool Football Club
LIVERPOOL versus LEICESTER CITY
31st JANUARY, 1981
Ticket and Match Information:
051-260 9999 (24 hour service)
PADDOCK ENCLOSURE
Row H   Seat No. 212
Match Sponsored by:
BOWYERS
A Division of Scot Bowyer Ltd.
This portion to be retained

Leicester City FOOTBALL CLUB
City Stadium, Filbert Street
Leicester LE2 7FL
Ticket and Match Enquiries
Leicester 551155 (24hr service)

* MATCH TICKETS Bookable two months in advance
* TICKET OFFICE Open Monday to Friday 10.00am to 5.00pm
* SATURDAYS Football Season 10.00am-1pm and after match for Advance Sales
* POSTAL APPLICATIONS Welcome, please enclose correct remittance and S.A.E

CITY V LIVERPOOL   SECTION WING STAND   BLOCK X
23RD AUGUST 1980
K.O. 3.00 PM   4805   PRICE 21   ROW £2.50 F   SEAT 9
LEAGUE DIVISION I

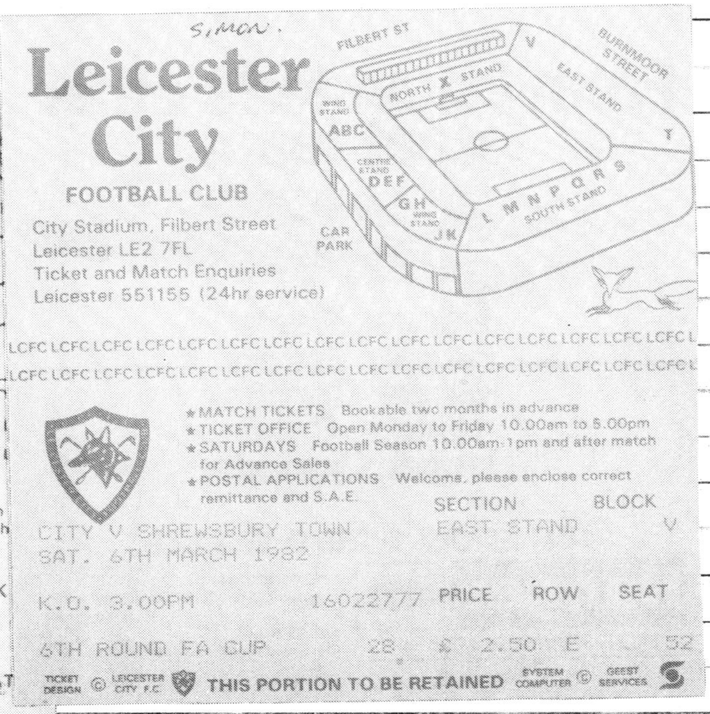

Leicester City FOOTBALL CLUB
Simon.
City Stadium, Filbert Street
Leicester LE2 7FL
Ticket and Match Enquiries
Leicester 551155 (24hr service)

* MATCH TICKETS Bookable two months in advance
* TICKET OFFICE Open Monday to Friday 10.00am to 5.00pm
* SATURDAYS Football Season 10.00am-1pm and after match for Advance Sales
* POSTAL APPLICATIONS Welcome, please enclose correct remittance and S.A.E.

CITY V SHREWSBURY TOWN   SECTION EAST STAND   BLOCK V
SAT. 6TH MARCH 1982
K.O. 3.00PM   16022777   PRICE 28   ROW £2.50 E   SEAT 52
6TH ROUND FA CUP

WEMBLEY STADIUM LIMITED
Football League Championship
Endsleigh Insurance League
1ST DIVISION PLAY-OFF
MONDAY 30TH MAY
KICK-OFF 1.30PM
TURNSTILES OPEN 11.30AM
TURNSTILE B
BLOCK 211 ROW 31 SEAT 164
£17.00
32100 857 110594 111216A

Leicester City FOOTBALL CLUB
City Stadium, Filbert Street
Leicester LE2 7FL
Ticket and Match Enquiries
Leicester City Clubcall 0898 121185 (24 hr. service)

MATCH TICKETS Bookable two months in advance
MEMBERS STAND Tickets sold only to season ticket holders or members card holders
FAMILY SEATING PACKAGE One or two juvenile seats at reduced price with every adult ticket purchased. Available in advance, booking only up to three hours before kick-off.
TICKET OFFICE Open Monday to Friday 10.00am to 5.00pm
SATURDAYS Football Season 10.00am - 12 noon and after match for Advance Sales
POSTAL APPLICATIONS Welcome, please enclose correct remittance and S.A.E
TELEPHONE BOOKINGS Accepted from Access and Visa credit card holders up to three hours before kick-off on Leicester 555000

CITY V OXFORD UNITED   SECTION MEMBERS WING   BLOCK J
SAT. 11th. MAY, 1991.   321005
KICK-OFF 3:00 PM   PRICE 3   ROW £7.00 B   SEAT 20
BARCLAYS L'GUE DIV.2

35

Bad

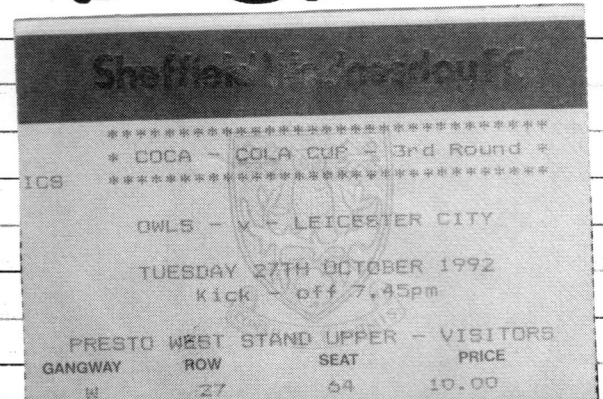

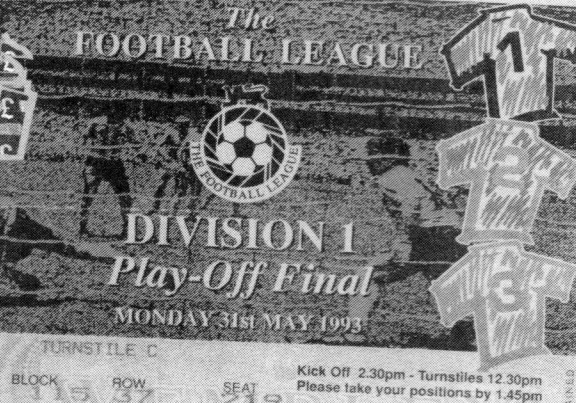

Tucked away among some more obvious thrashings, play-off defeats and crushing FA Cup exits is the City v Stoke ticket from 1985 which requires some further explanation... it was the dullest 0-0 draw I have ever seen, it was snowing and there was a bus strike which meant we had to walk the seven miles home in a raging blizzard.

Dennis Rofe Compassed

Cheeky, cheery, chipper cock-nee sparrer Dennis Rofe was one of my Filbert Street favourites, until he jumped ship half way through the 1979-80 Championship season, reckoning that Chelsea were a better bet for promotion. I was so enraged by this behaviour that in a voodoo style attack I set about my autographed Dennis Rofe 'Shoot!' poster with a compass and gave him a right slashing. This didn't appear to do the real Dennis any harm, which is more than can be said for my wallpaper. Don't mess with voodoo kids.

DENNIS ROFE
Leicester City

Meet your heroes...

Sue Riley has been meeting her heroes for years....
Circa 1981: A) There will always be a place for Sue on Larry May's knee. B) Sue and her pint just manage to get into this photo of a tender moment between Alan Young and Stewart Hamill. C) Alan Young again, impressing Sue with his big silver plate. D) Sue and that lovely fella Mark Wallington.

Sue is no fly-by-night however.... photo E) shows Sue, almost twenty years later, *still* having photos taken with the Filbo-related good and the great. In this case the goodest and greatest of them all.

More meetings...
F) Chris and Paul get to meet Steve Walsh, G) A clearly delighted Christian Vieri gets to meet Rob Coe. H) Steve Sims and Keith Weller get to meet Sue Williamson. I) Julian Joachim gets to meet Joan Sibson outside the North Stand toilets.

J) Peter Mays sent in this photo of Larry May, Tommy Williams and Dennis Rofe (sporting a cartoon-style 'shiner') meeting Bob Lambert and Ray Mays at a Rugby Branch 'do'. Using the 'tie-width system' Peter has managed to date this photo to approximately 'the height of the seventies'.

K) Chris Horner meets wing wizard Steve Guppy and insists, "No, he isn't wearing a fez with a hanky in it, it's a girl standing behind him."

L) Paulo Futre would have got to meet Rob Coe, if those damn fool Atletico fans hadn't got in the way.

M) Eddie Kelly (centre) meets team-mate Trevor Christie (right) and invites him to hold him in an upright position. We aren't sure who the chap on the left is, but we bet he's Eddie's 'Fuggin' bestest mate in all the world' at the moment.

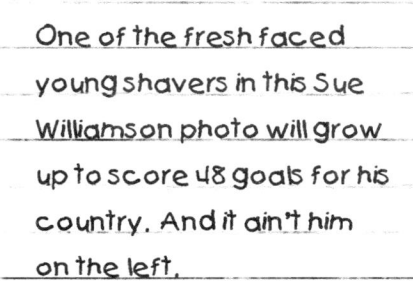

M.

One of the fresh faced young shavers in this Sue Williamson photo will grow up to score 48 goals for his country. And it ain't him on the left.

Oo-er look! It's that nice young man off the telly who does the sport on 'Midlands Today'. What's his name.... Ivor Gaskett? And what's that he's singing?

41

The Big Flick Off

Long time FOX cartoonist Simon Smith promised to venture up into his mother's attic where he had left a Subbuteo team customised to look like Jock's Foxes of 1980. There was even, Simon swore blind, a 'Paul Edmunds' with a bit of orange sponge stuck on his head to represent the young winger's fiery red bubble perm. When the distinctive light green box finally arrived in the post it was accompanied by a note which read: "Found the Subbuteo team, but has been tragically repainted into a mid-eighties Admiral shoulder stripe Ind Coope/John Bull strip... and I can't remember doing it, which is worrying. Anyway, the duckling haired one is obviously Simon Morgan; Ian Wilson will be the fair one with a bald bit on top; the gingerish No.10 is Ali Mauchlen; I can't remember if the one with the moustache is Ian Banks or Steve Lynex; No. 8 is either Tony

Sealy or Mark Bright; the black one is Laurie Cunningham; the one with a funny bit on top of his head is Russell Osman and the keeper is Ian Andrews, though the fact that one of his hands is missing may go some way to explaining his dip in form."

Please note also, Seventies Subbuteo-ites, the 'Corner kickers' box still has its original 'Sports Ltd' price tag of £0.30. A thrilling trip to that Belvoir Street grotto-of-all-things-sport is no longer an option for the current generation of keyboard prodders. They'll never know what they are missing. Actua Soccer indeed.

Andy Buckingham's Stars &

Andy Buckingham was the luckiest kid in the world. He lived on Burnmoor Street. Yes, look impressed. His gang's football pitch was the FILBERT STREET CAR PARK and it was all in a days work for the ten year old Andy to waylay City stars on the way home from training with his box brownie and commit them to film for all eternity. Not only that, but he got them signed too. I am weeping with jealousy as I scrawl this. I told my Mum we should move to Filbert Street...

their cars sixties collection

Those stars in full (from left to right top row): Tom Sweenie & his Hillman Imp; John Sjoberg & his Hillman Minx; David Gibson and his VW Beetle; Mike Stringfellow & his Triumph Herald. (bottom row) Clive Walker & his Cortina; Jackie Sinclair, waiting for a lift; Bobby Roberts, waiting for a bus; & finally... Matt Gillies - the Guv'nor, waiting for Andy to wind the film on.

It must be true... it

Yes, this was an actual genuine headline in The Sun in 1981 when, for a brief couple of days, Jock Wallace looked to have pulled off the transfer coup of the century.

In my scrapbook of the time, glued down in retrospect after the dust had settled, I put this article under the heading: 'Johan Cruyff for City? I don't think so.' in a sardonic, knowing sort of way. As if I hadn't really been charging round the living room shrieking with excitement when news of a possible deal was reported on *Midlands Today*, with Alan Towers. No sir, not me. Mark Wallington going to Ajax? When you think about it, it is the exact opposite of Cruyff coming to City. And just as likely. Ally, of 'Ally's Tartan Army' fame as new City manager? Thankfully for us he didn't seem quite such an attractive prospect after Scotland had played Iran and Peru in Argentina...

JOCK'S CRUYFF SWOOP

WALLACE... I have my man

JOHAN CRUYFF... could pick up £4,000 a game

by KEN LAWRENCE

JOHAN CRUYFF is today set for a sensational move to First Division strugglers Leicester City.

The Dutch Master has lined up a deal worth £4,000 a game for 11 matches—and if everything works out, he will make his debut against reigning European champions Nottingham Forest on Saturday.

Last night jubilant Leicester boss Jock Wallace insisted: "Johan and I have already agreed terms. He has one or two problems to sort out, but I am very hopeful he will join us on Thursday."

Cruyff is considering the move for two reasons. He must play competitive football to make his international comeback for Holland, and he wants to try out the English First Division before deciding on a one-year contract with Arsenal next season.

The one barrier to Leicester's transfer scoop lies with Spanish Second Division side Levante, who could make a late final bid.

They have had month-long talks with Cruyff, but last night the Dutchman indicated they are now too late although Leicester's activity could produce one last eleventh-hour effort.

Cruyff, who last played for Holland in 1977, wants to return against France in a World Cup qualifier on March 25.

Agreement

To be eligible he must first be playing in a national soccer league.

Because Levante have wasted so much time, Cruyff looks like he may plump for England, though by so doing he would lose £75,000 on any agreement with the Spanish club.

He told me: "I still like the idea of Spain, because the climate suits me and my family.

"But I cannot wait any longer for Levante. I want a guarantee from them and we have been negotiating for a month but every day they tell me a new story."

Wallace added: "I would like to think that part of Johan's interest is down to our personal friendship. I have known him since 1973 when he scored a fabulous goal for Ajax against Rangers when I was at Ibrox in the first European Super Cup.

"The negotiations have been going on by telephone over the past three to four weeks and now I think I have my man. He would teach my kids so much and be a great advert for Leicester City."

were in the paper

THURSDAY, FEBRUARY 22, 1979

AJAX WATCH CITY GOALKEEPER

LEICESTER CITY manager Jock Wallace, confirming that Dutch aces Ajax have made an approach for Mark Wallington, says he will not stand in the goalkeeper's way if the Amsterdam club follow up with a firm offer.

The initial inquiry is the first certain news of interest in the former England Under-23 keeper, although several other clubs have been linked with a deal.

Said Wallace: "Ajax came on to ask where they could see Mark in action in the next week or so but we haven't got to the stage of talking about price or anything yet.

"The big fellow has stated both privately and publicly that he wants a transfer and his request was granted. He's an experienced professional so it is up to him to make the most of his chances.

"If he wants to go then he's better away. But I have great respect for the player. At the start of the season he kept us alive with some fantastic displays.

Speculation

"It's just a pity he wants to leave when our young team is on the way up. But, good luck to him. I hope he gets his wish. There's no point in keeping a player who wants to leave."

A price of £250,000 has been speculated and there is no doubt that Wallace values Wallington in the six-figure bracket. Perhaps that figure is slightly high for a Second Division player from a club not yet bidding for promotion.

And, even if the clubs agree terms, will the player go. Wallington said today: "I'm very flattered at the interest of such a great club as Ajax. They are one of the sides you dream about joining.

by Bill Anderson

"But, it would be silly to take the view that it would be the same as joining an English club. It raises a bigger question on family matters, like schooling for my kids and language problems.

"At the moment, I am intrigued at the prospect and I will do my best, as always, for City. Until Ajax make a firm offer and then discuss terms with me, there's nothing much I can say. But I think that I would go."

With City's current back four already established as the basis of the new-look team, Wallace could go in to his own ranks for a replacement with Sean Rafter and youngsters Steve Humphries and Paul Easson competing for the place.

Incidentally, one of the reasons behind the surprising approach from Ajax is that the Filbert Street tent has guaranteed all the home fixtures since the turn of the year.

Televised English games are beamed to the Continent, where our game is rated higher than the home product, so Dutch viewers have been able to see some fine displays by Wallington.

Lucrative

This T.V. shop window may now result in a big-money transfer for City as well as a lucrative deal for Wallington, but much will depend on his next few performances.

Ajax officials will put him under the microscope against Charlton on Saturday and later in the Cup tie at Oldham on Monday, subject to both games beating the weather.

MARK WALLINGTON... "I think I would go."

LEICESTER GO FOR MacLEOD

Exclusive... By Norman Wynne

ALLY MACLEOD could make a sensational return to club management when he comes back from the World Cup in Argentina in July.

The man who will guide Scotland's hopes in South America is wanted by relegated Leicester to get them back into the First Division.

Last night MacLeod said: "At the moment all I want to think about is Scotland and the World Cup. Nothing else."

Leicester know that MacLeod, 47, would never consider giving up the chance to go to Argentina. But they are prepared to wait until his return and then make him the kind of offer he could find difficult to refuse.

He's made no secret in the past that he'd like to try English football management.

Danger

● The next World Cup is in danger already! It's due for Spain in four years time and even now there is trouble in the air. There is a proposal that there should be 24 qualifiers for the final stages, primarily to accomodate the smaller African countries.

UEFA, however, are not prepared to accept it. President, Dr. Artemio Franchi, has made it clear they wanted no interference from the smaller nations who want more active participation in the World Cup.

The South American countries feel the same way and future World Cups could be between Europe and South America.

ALLY MACLEOD

Scarf-ace

LEICESTER
"CHANT"
SILK SCARF
65p
(70p post paid)

Sometime during the early 1970's the football scarf changed its primary function. It turned from being a warm, woolly way of keeping the cold out during those winter matches whilst at the same time displaying your allegiance, into a testing ground for every new technological fabric printing breakthrough known to man.

Smoothed out into the Big Blue Scrapbook here are my trusty old woollen bar scarf - the universal sign for 'football supporter' on television and in cartoons..... a 'Chant silk-scarf', to be tied around the wrist after the fashion of the day, which has a sort of white plastic printed on to scratchy polyester and is slowly turning from royal blue to purple..... and both sides of a 'photo scarf' designed more for your wall than your neck.

It appears that the woollen scarf has made a bit of comeback lately, although trends towards 'Filbert the Fox' and Tottenham Hotspur navy blue should not be encouraged.

The Knitwear Motel

When the cry for scrap to fill the Big Blue Scrapbook first went out in The FOX we weren't sure what the response would be. Then this newspaper cutting arrived from Paul Jackson with the following note attached...

"It's a cracking idea, and every success with the Big Blue Scrapbook. Why I kept this I'll never know, but Birch looks great in his tank top and Keith is wearing a seriously with-it cardie. However, Denise the waitress is looking a little crumpled after bumping into Franky Wortho on the way to the sweet trolley..."

No complaints from Leicester stars Keith Weller (left) and Alan Birchenall as Denise Panter serves lunch in their luxury motel.

LEICESTER CITY, who splashed out £300,000 to sign Jon Sammels, Alan Birchenall and Keith Weller earlier this season, are facing a further outlay of around £2,000.

That is what it is costing the club to house their expensive stars until accommodation of their own can be occupied.

Sammels, who moved from Arsenal in July, stayed at a luxury motel not far from City's Filbert Street ground for two months. The bill? Around £75 a week.

Alan Birchenall followed at the end of September from Crystal Palace and is still there. Keith Weller bought from Chelsea, joined him a week later.

Sammels has now moved out, but Leicester still get a weekly bill of £150 for Birchenall and Weller.

Says Leicester secretary John Smith:

"We have our own hostels, but senior professionals deserve something better.

"Obviously it helps a player if he lives in the kind of surroundings that appeal to him. We reap our reward on the field.

49

The 'It's War!' Semi-final

City in an FA Cup Semi Final and a bally war breaking out on the same day? There's a weekend we won't forget. This copy of The Sun from Saturday April 3rd 1982 has both events covered. The gleeful front page 'IT'S WAR' headline was held up to car windows on the way to Villa Park to taunt the Spurs fans who had Argentinians Ardiles and Villa in their side. Sadly the back page article 'Cocky Jock's Double Talk', as well as the car sticker 'Jock's Foxes Eat Cockerels' proved to be a tad over-optimistic as City lost 2-0. On the way home the Spurs fans held up photos of own-goal scorer Ian Wilson from the programme... CURSES!!

Does anyone want to buy a set of adult size tracksuits? Cheap?

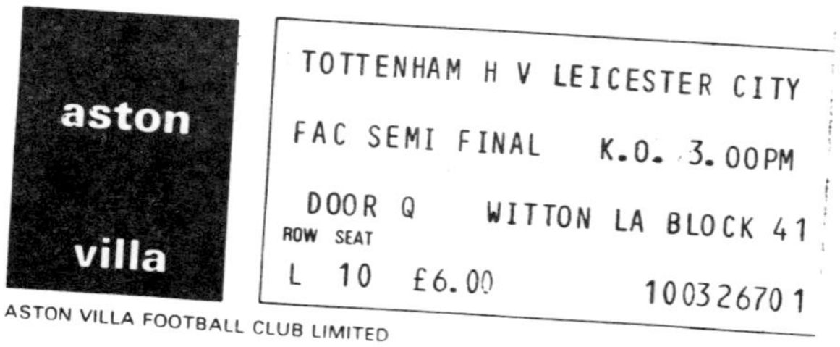

COCKY JOCK'S DOUBLE TALK

By ROGER DUCKWORTH

LEICESTER manager Jock Wallace, who led mighty Rangers to three Scottish Cup and League doubles before leaving for Filbert Street, thundered last night: "We are going to be another Rangers — an English version."

Then, Wallace not only forecast a Leicester win over Spurs at Villa Park today, but he calmly said: "I just happen to think we will win the Cup and get promotion, too."

Unchanged

But big Jock admitted he would like to strengthen his team. "I have no money though and the club needs whatever we earn. So I can't have it for players.

"Whatever happens at Villa Park we will have a few days off. I would like to take the lads to Majorca, but we just can't afford it."

As he named an unchanged team, Wallace admitted his feelings for supersub Jim Melrose. "He has done wonders for us and scored a lot of goals. But he went out with an injury and since then we have had a great run."

Jock knows his Leicester youngsters won't come second in the fitness stakes today.

Shifts

"We did our hard work in the dead of winter, coming back every afternoon for gym work and circuits. We did more afternoon shifts than the local factories."

Last word from the last line of defence, keeper and skipper Mark Wallington who said: "I have to fancy us. The atmosphere in our dressing-room is marvellous."

MARK WALLINGTON . . . "I have to fancy us."

JOCK WALLACE . . gives lads a few days off

Off the tracks

LEICESTER have lost the tracksuit tops the players were to have worn for today's FA Cup semi-final against Spurs at Villa Park.

The club was raided when thieves squeezed through a small window — but only the tops were stolen. Manager Jock Wallace has asked the manufacturers for replacements.

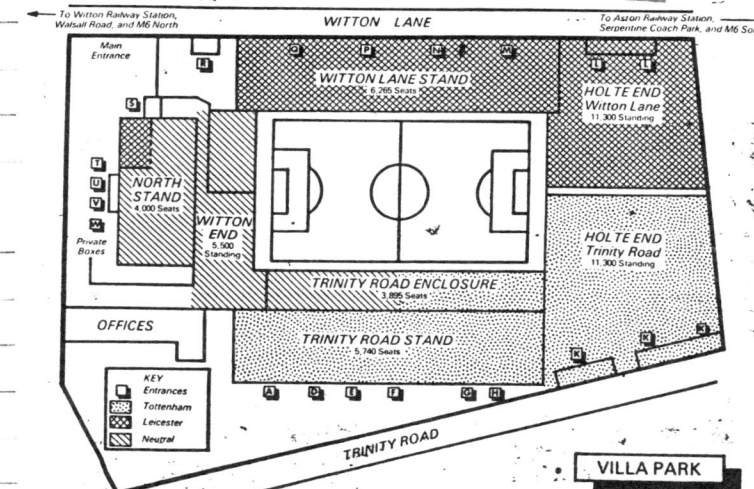

OWN GOAL KILLED US — JOCK

IAN WILSON will for some time relive the nightmare moment in the 76th minute when his intended pass back to 'keeper Mark Wallington sailed in to the net and sealed Leicester's FA Cup fate. "It was the killer," admitted disappointed manager Jock Wallace after seeing his Second Division battlers succumb to an attack of the Wembley wobbles.

F.A. CUP: Semi-finals

TOTTENHAM (0) ....2 LEICESTER (0) 0
Crooks, Wilson o.g.   (46,606 at Villa Park.
                          Receipts £211,108)

Q.P.R. (0) ....1 WEST BROM (0) 0
Allen   (45,015 at Highbury)

51

Doing Penance

This comprehensive collection of City pennants comes to you courtesy of Sue Williamson's heaving attic collection. Apart from the 'Farewell to the Main Stand' one which I have to hold my hand up to. There's always a buck to be made out of sentimental fools.

This City pennant (below) formed the centre-piece of a football exhibition in a service station on the outskirts of Norrkoping in Sweden. Why, we don't know. But it's the sort of thing you like to see when you are many miles from home...

David Speedie... Good or Evil?

The name David Speedie can cause conflicting emotions within the heart of any City fan. What comes to mind first? His dive in Blackburn Rovers' yellow at Wembley in 1992... or his battling contribution to City's promotion in 1993-94? Arch Cov City hater Simon Kimber recalls a day when Speedie managed to ruin his day before either of these events...

"We went to a wedding on the day that City lost 4-2 to Sheff Wednesday in September 1990. Not only did I have to miss a City home match (I didn't know then that Mike Hooper would be letting in four goals) but the Sky Blue Scum were at the same hotel as the wedding. Cyrille Regis, George Curtis, Speedie, Schnoz, the whole bloody circus. The photographer recognised them and swiftly roped Speedie & Co into the photos... I was the only other person at the wedding who had the slightest clue who the hell they were. What a bloody awful way to spend a Saturday afternoon.."

On the other hand the Speedster did have his charming side. When The FOX interviewed him

just after he had arrived at Leicester we had to wait until he had tenderly signed an autograph for a young City fan. Aaaahhhhh. Then again, you still got the feeling that he would gnaw your face off if you happened to ask him a question that he didn't like....
And the Speedometer did miss Wembley '94 for City after scrapping with Tramnmere players in the Play Off Semi Final...
but he did score in that game...
but he didn't actually touch the ball on its way into the net...
but he did stay at Leicester for the Premiership season of 94-95....
but he didn't actually play a single game because he was injured all season...
and he did become a player's agent...
David Speedie Good or Evil? You decide...

The Best of What a Card!

The FOX's predecessor to the Big Blue Scrapbook was Derek Hammond's 'What a Card!' series. Here are some Saturday evening edited highlights...

ROFE Can you spot the amusing comedy error smuggled into this 1978 *Sun Soccercard* selection by the fun-loving artist?

KELLY No, we don't mean the error he made in staying up to crayon in the entire 1000 card series all in one night.

KEMBER And no, it isn't the fact that each of these alleged City team-mates has pulled on a completely different version of the hallowed royal blue nylon.

SIMS Not a mistake; this is in fact a superb likeness of Tommy Williams, not a crap Steve Sims. And, incidentally, Steve Kember's gob was all sideways like that in real life.

DAVIES Yes, of course Roger Davies was a tragically stupid mistake; but you can't lay the blame for Big Rog at the door of a talentless *Sun* bloke with a felt-pen.

HUGHES Hmm, Billy Hughes looks like he's got his suspicions. He's spotted the clue on the back of the Alan Hoult card, where it says he's just been transferred to Bristol Rovers, without ever making the first-team at "the Filbert Road club"...

HOULT That's correct, guys 'n' gals!?! On this ultimately collectable Soccercard, the cheeky *Sun* artist has replaced the head of Bristol Rovers striker Alan Hoult (Leicester City) with that of former popular once fashionable Radio One DJ Steve Wright in the Afternoon!

THE Sun SOCCERCARDS
STRIKERS
831

ALAN HOULT
(Leicester City)

Schoolboy joining Leicester City and signing professional in September, 1975. Yet Alan was not given a League game by the Filbert Road club. Had a months loan with both Hull City and Lincoln City and scored a goal with both clubs. Bristol Rovers had been impressed with his skill in the Leicester Reserves and when given a free transfer in the summer of 1978 was signed by Rovers.

YOUNG/GOODWIN In this *Panini 80* sticker set, City players were forced to share a card 'cos we were in the old Second Division. Here, cocky young Mark Goodwin dares to pull a surly face, safe in the knowledge no one will go and poke him in the eye when he's on the same card as Alan Young 'cos Alan Young's hard.

BYRNE/HENDERSON This pair ended up together because no one else fancied sharing with either of the useless buggers. Paddy Byrne had luminous white legs, and Henderson was snapped up by his old boss Jock Wallace on the iffy grounds of him having won the Chilly Jocko Championship for Rangers. Johan Cruyff might've been a better bet.

FRANKIE/WORTHO No-one's fit to share this *Soccer Stars 76-77* card with the great Frank Worthington. He is so cool - Don Rogers of Crystal Palace is chuffed just to get a sneaky look-in in Wortho's photographic slipstream.

WOOLLETT/THE BULLET Alan Woollett looks a bit perturbed, primarily because Keith Weller's always giggling at his bottom as he's trotting out of the tunnel.

ROFE/STEVENS An ideal couple. Ex-Ranger 'Gregor' is free to cook and dust and put the hoover round while Dennis is out earning a crust, playing football for Leicester City.

WILLIAMS/MAY That's enough crap 'cardshare' jokes... for the time being.

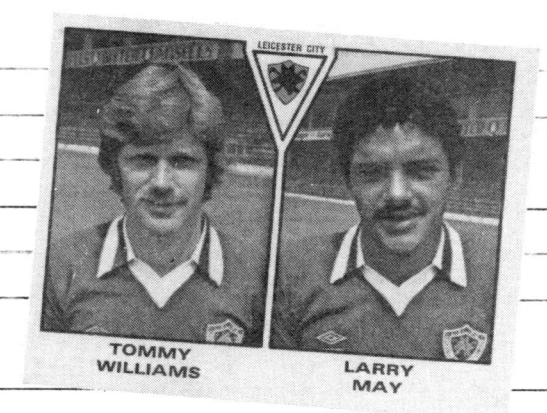

STEVE WALSH A couple of insulting gems from last season's frankly amateurish *ProMatch Series 2*. For a start, it's no wonder that this barrel-chested, love-handled Walshie only scores 64% on the 'speed' scale. But only 72% for temperament? There isn't a single City fan, armchair expert or Premier striker in the country who'd doubt Steve is, as ever, ONE HUNDRED PERCENT! And that's plus all the points he's picked up for taking the piss out of Steve Bull over the years...

NEIL LENNON Walshie may look fat on his card, but at least he didn't end up resembling a cross between Beavis & Butthead and/or an axe murderer. *ProMatch* make up in part for these crimes, and for scoring our Neil ridiculously low in the 'positioning' (78%) and 'stamina' (85%) stakes by uncannily capturing his trademark 'Roadrunner'

BRYAN HAMILTON - IPSWICH TOWN Here's useless ex-City boss Hamilton on the day he somehow managed to land the Northern Ireland job. No wonder he's looking chipper - it's the first time he's had reason to smile for nine years, ever since he pinched us Walshie off Wigan for three shillings and sixpence!

THUR LITTLE LYAH - VILLA "Howay Thelma pet, ah sweer on the Hurly Bible ah nevvah had nur hur-mur-sexual Jur-annah Lumleh burl hairdur when ah wus a pleeyah at owah football club. That big mushrurm thing on mah heed? Ah sweer it's a canny flared murtahcycle helmet, man lad..."

MARK McGHEE - CELTIC Thanks to FOX reader Dean Gale for sending this McGhee card along with a cheap jibe about him having walked out on the Hoops when the size of his expanding gut called for the slimming stripes of Newcastle. McGhee is pictured walking out of his own *Mirror 88* sticker, having heard of an unmissable photo-opportunity elsewhere in the album.

SID VICIOUS - F****T How hilarious - it's Martin O'Neill looking *slightly* younger!?!

ARTHUR POTTER (Weller Card) "I say, to think we're missing the bloody wrestling, eh?", jests Mr Arthur Potter (rear left - car coat, large crimplene tie and sideboards) in his annoyingly loud voice, attracting the attention of fully two-thirds of the other blokes standing in the Filbert Street End. "To think we're missing the wrestling to come and see this bloody shower, eh?" Mercifully, the great Keith Weller is limbering up just out of earshot.

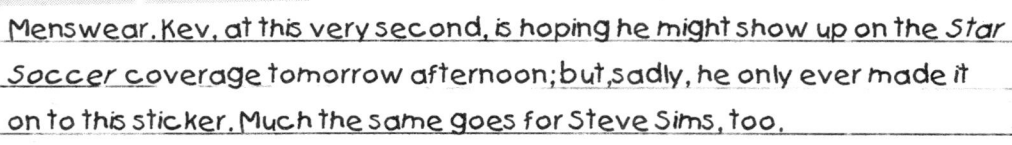

KEVIN COSGROVE (Sims Card) That's Kev - the one on the front row with the triangular trousers and the too-small snorkel parka from Irish Menswear. Kev, at this very second, is hoping he might show up on the *Star Soccer* coverage tomorrow afternoon; but, sadly, he only ever made it on to this sticker. Much the same goes for Steve Sims, too.

STEVE EARLE Those Admiral tracky tops really were the bee's knees weren't they? A fashion flash-forward to the totally kickin' techno raver gear of the present day. Big up! For bitchin' Steve Earle of the speed-garage junglist massive...

REG TOMPKINS (Birch Card) Talking of ravers, here's the Birch warming up for City just three hours after being kicked out of the Friday all-niter at *Bailey's* - "the most swinging 'n' sophisticated discotheque within chundering distance of the Clock Tower." As you can see, Birch has just proved his match fitness by successfully walking Jimmy Bloomfield's special white line. "Allegedly", adds Mr Reg Tompkins (trilby hat, bottom left) to his delightful, dishy daughter, Sherry.

ALAN BIRCHENALL Here's Birch emerging, Mork From Ork-style, out of a giant white & blue egg. But don't be 'eggs-asperated'. Our favourite half-time spirits-lifter isn't going to 'whisk' himself off to some 'eggstraterrestial' planet. It's just a case of dodgy artwork in the cheapest and nastiest-ever set of soccer stickers. When FKS couldn't find a head-and-shoulders of a player in his current club colours, they pulled the old trick of simply crayoning (or, in our case, Tippexing) over an old mugshot. And Alan Birchenall (Crystal Palace) was one of the better bodge-jobs in their 1973-74 'album-en'!

FRANK WORTHINGTON Another out-size blob of Tippex directed at Frank's Huddersfield Town stripes. And well done again to FKS's painstaking research department, for crayoning the City 'club colour' flag a traditional black & white...

59

BIRCH'S EXISTENTIAL AGONY Think 'Birch', and the chances are you think of the cheeky, chirpy, chappie cheering us up at half-time with a useless joke, a spin of the semi-celebrity tombola and a cheap jibe at the oppo fans crunched into their crappy corner over in the Pop Side. Yet beneath the effervescent exterior, there lies the heavy weight of Birch's manifold wordly concerns - the impending end of youth; the growing popularity of women's lib; the plight of the bottle-nosed dolphin - have quite literally brought him to his knees, or at least his arse.

BIRCH AGAINST THE FURIOUS ELEMENTS A bitter wind blows freezing drizzle into the sparse crowd, making even the most ardent City fans yearn for respite, and half-time Bovril. But out on the pitch, there is no umbrella to shield young Birch from the full horror of the furious elements. Stinking black mud clings to his shorts; the rain plasters down his hair, soaking through to the very core of his soul. *Soccer Stars 72-73* - a collectable card highly prized among miserable football ephemera specialists.

WOE IS BIRCH We find Birch in *deadly* serious action on this *Topps 1975* card. As he lunges hopelessly for the ball, which this afternoon seems forever just out of reach, Birch secretly longs for the end of the game, and the end of this pitiful search for *approval* and *meaning*. As his panting breath catches in his throat and sweat prickles his back, Birch looks forward only to a vacuous night out on the pull at Bailey's bistrotheque on the Clocktower, where he will attempt to find momentary solace in the arms of Sherry, a Wigstonian in a crocheted poncho.

THE PAIN OF IT ALL The *A&BC* photographer homes in unforgivably on that which the *Sun Soccercard* snapper chose to overlook: the bitter tears flowing down the cheeks of the beautiful young Birch. To a casual onlooker, the rich, successful soccer star has the world at his feet. Meanwhile, the demons in Birch's tortured mind never let him escape a creeping sense of futility. The inevitability of the Apocalypse. The millions of lonely children in the world. And that second helping of chicken madras Peter Osgood served him up last night, giving it the large one on the piss at Gitanji's of Mayfair...

The Green Green Grass at Home

Who can honestly say they haven't, at some time or other, felt the urge to take a bit of Filbert Street home with them? Or is it just me? This treasured clod of turf was removed from the Double Decker end penalty area by myself during the 'Great Escape' pitch invasion of 1991. As soon as I got home I stuck it in a corner of the lawn. It soon began to thrive and expand and, being of a far superior quality to the rest of the lawn, to TAKE OVER producing a largish patch of deep rich green putting the rest of the lawn to shame.

LEICESTER		CAMBRIDGE
Carl Muggleton	1.	John Vaughan
Gary Mills	2.	Mick Heathcote
Mike Whitlow	3.	Alan Kimble
Colin Hill	4.	Tony Dennis
Steve Walsh	5.	Phil Chapple
Tony James	6.	Danny O'Shea
Steve Thompson	7.	Michael Cheetham
Simon Grayson	8.	Richard Wilkins
Tommy Wright	9.	Dion Dublin
Ian Ormondroyd	10.	Steve Claridge
Kevin Russell	11.	Lee Philpott
David Oldfield	12.	Micky Norbury
Phil Gee	14.	Paul Gaync...

Ref. Martin Bodenham (Cornwall).

Simon Kimber has also known how it feels to walk off with anything Filbo-related that wasn't screwed down. After the glorious play-off semi-final win of 1992 that saw City destroy Cambridge United 5-0 he was sitting near the pressbox in the old Wing Stand and could not resist reaching over and nicking the journalist's team sheet pinned to the back wall. It was a crime of passion your honour.

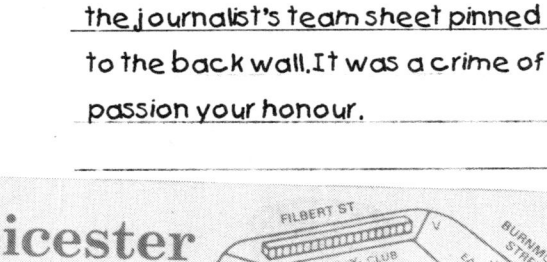

Leicester City Football Club — City Stadium, Filbert Street, Leicester LE2 7FL — City v Cambridge United, Wednesday 13th May 1992, Kick-off 7:45 PM, Division 2 Play-off — Members Wing, Price £7.50

Matt Warrington's

Matt Warrington from County Mayo already had his own Big Blue Scrapbook, charting City's progress all the way to Wembley in the 1969 FA Cup, and he sent it across the water to us. If anyone has any further adventures of 'Stoopid' the City-supporting dog from the Sports Mercury, we'd really like to see them.

Last-gasp Leicester goal ko's the Cu[p]

'GOLDEN BOY' CL[ARKE] SEES CITY THRO[UGH]

West Bromwich Albion 0 Leicester 1

LEICESTER CITY, a club haunted by relegation fears, are through to Wembley. A 53,207 crowd packed into Hillsborough and saw £150,000 Allan Clarke, Leicester controversial star, score the goal four minutes from the end of this F.A. Cup semi-final which was like a bayonet thrust to West Brom's throat.

by **ALAN HOBY**

Clarke hoisted manager Frank O'Farrell's Midland underdogs into the Final with the most important goal of his mercurial career.

In the most dramatic finale I have seen for a long time, in an otherwise tense and nervy struggle, Leicester's substitute Malcolm Manley, who had come on in the second-half for the injured Len Glover (damaged groin), swung over the ball.

Andy Lochhead, Leicester's towering striker who had duelled grimly and physically with Albion centre half John Talbut, headed down. There was a moment of stillness and then Clarke brought his right foot down on the ball from around the edge of the box.

COLLAPSED

Low and hard it sped across the sandied muddy pitch. And then, amid a tumultuous howl of joy from the Leicester thousands, the ball flashed inside the post and into the net with John Osborne, West Brom's diving keeper, clutching nothing but thin air.

The scene as Leicester scored, just when a goalless draw seemed certain, was one to warm every City heart.

Their blue-shirted players cavorted, danced, and flung themselves about in delight. But even more dramatic was the scene in the next few electrical minutes.

● **Well hello there!** Leicester pivot John Sjoberg ends up with his arms round 'keeper Peter Shilton's neck after foiling Albion's [...] (white) in the [...]

Allan Clarke collapsed clutching his knee. Leicester's hero was, it seemed, badly hurt.

As the crowd watched, and the Albion players fidgeted with impatience, Clarke was carried off by O'Farrell and Leicester physiotherapist George Preston, his face twisted with pain.

The moments that followed, including four minutes of injury time, were sheer agonising suspense for Leicester fans.

So taut were the nerves of the Leicester team that once when little Asa Hartford lashed out at the ball in desperation, only to kick Leicester 'keeper Peter Shilton, a menacing throng of blue shirts closed in on him.

But tempers cooled and finally referee Ray Tinkler, who had kept tight control on a struggle which at times threatened to boil over, whistled the end of this far from classic semi-final.

Afterwards O'Farrell told me that fears concerning Clarke's injury could be dispelled.

"Glover's damaged groin," he told me, "is the more serious, and he will not be fit for our vital League match at Coventry on Tuesday.

"Clarke had to go off because the pain at that point was so intense that he couldn't carry on. But I expect him to be fit for the Coventry game."

'DELIGHTED'

Commenting on Clarke's golden goal, O'Farrell said: "I'm delighted, of course. But I'm particularly delighted Allan scored the goal. He has been subjected to some adverse publicity which he shouldn't have got."

O'Farrell, who has now been manager for three months, added: "This is the first shot Allan has hit properly for the last weeks. He's been topping them or not hitting them right. He was obviously saving it all up for today."

"Relegation? We don't [...]"

● Top, Albion 'keeper John Osborne lies beaten by Cl[arke] [...] away in triumph as the Albion d[...]

HEROES

Leicester can thank their tall, efficient defenders. Joe Sjoberg and that man for all crises, Graham Cross. Other Leicester heroes were their captain David Nish, only 21, Peter Rodrigues, their right-back who sank on to the turf at the end as if in prayer, and Bobby Roberts, whose workrate was quite fantastic.

But for the most part fear put a damp hand on this disappointing game—the fear of losing.

There was little of the usual semi-final emotion until those last stirring minutes.

Then Lochhead at last escaped the rugged attentions of Talbut to give Allan Clarke that wonderful opportunity to pay off his fantastic fee.

I felt sorry for Graham Lovett, Albion's clever linkman, but the [...]

SCOREBOARD
CITY — 1
W. Brom. — 0
CLARKE (A) (City)
87 mins.
Official attendance: 53,207
Receipts: £47,500

Cup Run Scrapbook

olders

RKE
JGH

● City hero Allan Clarke (left) is congratulated by Andy Lochhead after the game.

Below, Lochhead (9) and Clarke turn in misery.

HILLSBOROUGH

"This is high, Stoopid, and now we can look down towards Wembley again."

SHEFFIELD WED
HILLSBOROU

FOOTBALL ASSOCIATION CHALLENGE CUP
SEMI - FINAL
Saturday, 22nd March
KICK-OFF 3-0 p.m.

General Manager and Secretary
RESERVED SEAT 40/-

Issued subject to the Rules, Regulations and Bye-Laws of the Football Association. No Tickets exchanged nor money refunded. THIS PORTION

ENTRANCE **G**
GANGWAY **2**
To the RIGHT
ROW **R** SEAT **13**

YOU ARE REQUESTED TO TAKE UP YOUR POSITION

63

Peter Shilton Forever!

If Cliff Richards is the Peter Pan of Pop then what does that make Peter Shilton?! The Peter Pan of er... football. In his One Hundred year career Peter has done it all. He brought out his very own 'Peter Shilton's Football Annual' which told the 'Peter Shilton Story' from a Peter Shilton viewpoint. He invented his own all white 'PS' Admiral kit. He played for England a thousand times. He got fed up with Leicester and left for Stoke. He got to hang about with John Noakes on Blue Peter. He won the European Cup with Forest, but we don't talk about that. He made his millionth league appearance for Orient... And then there was the story of 'Peter Shilton's Amazing Betting Tash'... 1) This A&BC series from the Swinging Sixties featured an early, raggedy bumfluff version of the Shilton tash, mercifully somewhat out of focus. On the reverse of the card, it says its owner "seems a certainty for the 1970 World Cup". Shilts Form Guide: "Stick a few bob on this tash not lasting the season out. 4-1 at Coral's seems pretty generous to me. And I've already put my house on me getting the World Cup job at 2-1. Banksy's past it and we all know that Peter Bonetti couldn't catch a cold. Running Total: Minus one house and three shillings. 2) The rest of the City team didn't get on cards in the 70-71 2nd Division season, but Peter nicked in on one of the black & white photo jobbies that came free with every pack. Note thickening of tash and successful control of kinky barnet. Shilts' Form Guide: "Ee, I look like a young Valentino. But I'd still put a couple of quid on me going for the clean-shaven look now it's the seventies. I've got the inside track from Rodney Fern - long hair's going out of fashion y'know. And if I were you I'd

The Peter Shilton Story

IF YOU WANT TO GET TO THE TOP IN FOOTBALL THEN FOLLOW THE EXAMPLE OF **PETER SHILTON**! SATURDAYS HAVE ALWAYS BEEN EAGERLY AWAITED BY PETER. AS A YOUNG BOY HE WOULD TURN OUT FOR HIS PRIMARY SCHOOL IN THE MORNINGS AND SPEND ALL AFTERNOON IN THE PARK PLAYING FRIENDLY MATCHES WITH OTHER BOYS. PETER JUST COULDN'T GET ENOUGH SOCCER!

PETER ENJOYED SAVING GOALS ...AND SCORING THEM!

PETER DIDN'T SPEND ALL HIS TIME IN GOAL. HE BEGAN PLAYING FOR LEICESTER SCHOOLBOYS AT RIGHT BACK. BY THE TIME PETER WAS OLD ENOUGH TO GO TO SECONDARY SCHOOL SOCCER WAS ALL HE WANTED TO KNOW, BUT WHEN HE TURNED UP FOR HIS FIRST SPORTS SESSION PETER WAS LOST FOR WORDS. THE SCHOOL ONLY PLAYED **RUGBY!** PETER WAS SO UPSET HIS FATHER CONSIDERED MOVING HIM TO A NEW SCHOOL! JUST IN TIME THE SPORTSMASTER DECIDED TO FORM A FOOTBALL TEAM AND PETER WAS SAVED! BACK IN AN OLDER LEICESTER BOYS TEAM, PETER REACHED THE FINALS OF THE **ENGLISH SCHOOLS TROPHY.**

PETER'S PERFORMANCES IN GOAL THROUGHOUT THE COMPETITION BROUGHT HIM TO THE ATTENTION OF THE INTERNATIONAL SCHOOLBOY SELECTORS. PETER WON HIS **FIRST CAP,** FOR ENGLAND AGAINST EIRE. PETER IS STILL JUST AS PROUD OF HIS FIRST CAP AS ANY OTHER HONOURS HE HAS WON SINCE THAT FIRST INTERNATIONAL!

stick a fiver on that autograph being real." Running Total: Minus one house, seven pounds and fifteen new pence.

3) It's 1971-72, and we're up again! Against all the odds, Peter has grown some rather splendid facial furniture, has wantonly let his kink grow out... and he's gone for a Pancho Villa! Shilts' Form Guide: "I really dig this Pancho Villa look, I'll have another fiver on me keeping the tash like this for years if you'll give me evens. You've got to speculate to accumulate, eh? I saw this local band last night, sort of cabaret rock 'n' roll with Dion Dublin's Dad on sax, and I gave him 200-1 on them getting a number one single in the next five years. The sucker put a tenner on it! Running Total: Minus one house and £2,012.15. 4) See how smug Peter is now he's finally done the decent thing and ditched the demon tash for 73-74. The decision has clearly removed a weight from his shoulders, not to mention his top lip. The way is now clear for him to become an international grooming idol of the seventies, what with that revived kink and those attractive earmuffs. Shilts' Form Guide: "What a smasher! There's no way a bloke as lovely as me, with all those England caps, could ever fall on hard times. If things got tough I'd just apply for the City manager's job. I'd put my shirt on the board bending over backwards to get me back to Filbert Street." Total: The Hipster Tipster scores minus one house, minus £2,012.15, minus three shirts... and counting.

Origami Fox from Rupert Annual

'Steve the Nottingham Blue' is a City spy who lives among Forest fans and then reports back to us on how upset they are down the pub. He has devoted his life to hating Forest, and calls them 'Notts Forest' no matter how many times they tell him that 'Notts' is wrong. Steve sent us these origami fox instructions ripped out of a very old 'Rupert the Bear' annual and told us: 'I've tried it and it really works...' Expect to see them placed strategically around Nottingham, possibly housing listening devices.

Use a 5" to 7" square of paper white on one side black (or brown) on the other. Always check your fold in the next diagram.

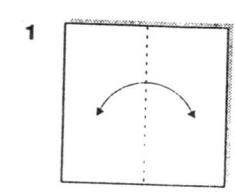

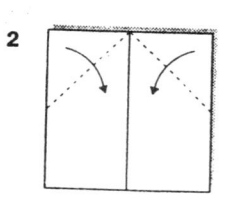

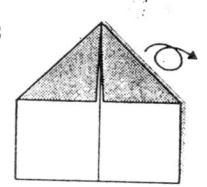

(1) White side up. Fold in half. Unfold. (2) Fold corners to centre line. (3) Turn model over - like turning a page in a book.

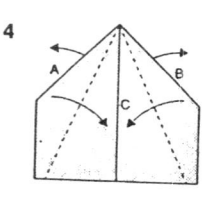

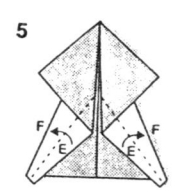

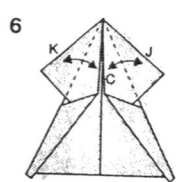

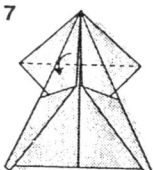

(4) Fold so edge 'A' lies along centre line 'C' let the flap underneath come out. Now do the same with 'B'. (5) Fold edge 'E' along 'F'.(both sides) (6) Fold edge 'J' along centre line 'C' and *open up* do the same with 'K' (7) Fold along dashed line.

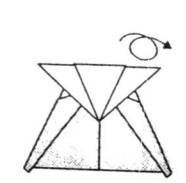

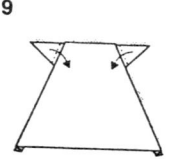

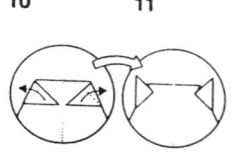

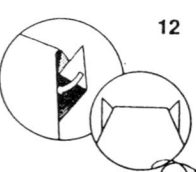

(8) Turn over like a page in a book. (9) Fold little flaps (ears) on dashed line. (10) Now fold the corners out again on dashed line. (11) This is the result now lift each ear and tuck *under* the top layer. (12) This is the ear being tucked under - do both now turn over.

(13) Fold up and crease on dashed line (about 1/3 of the way to the nose of the fox). (14) Hold each leg *below* the fold you made in step 13. Twist a little so your thumbs are on top and fingers below, now move the hands away from each other so the paper is tight - then bring the hands closer and Freddy will nod. (15) Move fingers together and then pull first one leg and then the other downwards, Freddy will put his head on one side.

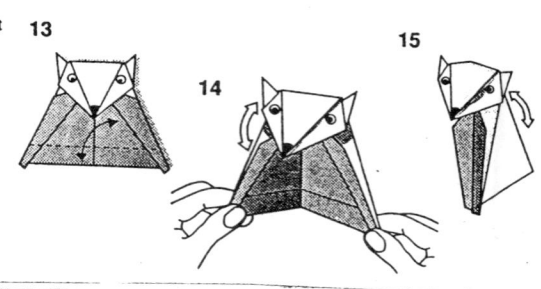

Medallions, man

They're chunky, they're funky, they're made by 'Coffer Sports' and they nestle in your chest hair in the large 'V' shape created by your open-to-the-waist denim shirt. At least they will when you grow some.

66

The Garry Lynaker Mis-spelling collection...

Paul Henderson sent us in a photocopy of his 'unusual but never far from interesting' collection.... the name 'Gary Lineker' spelt wrong on the team line-ups in programmes. Paul says he likes to imagine the faces of the embarrassed programme editors when they think of how famous Gary became.... and how they couldn't spell his name properly.

"1) Appeared in the City v Norwich FA Cup game from January 1979. An unforgivable double whammy spelling both christian name and surname wrong... considering that it was a home programme. 2) Is from a Fulham away match in February 1980. We'll let them off with a slapped wrist as young Gary Linek-Ear was yet to burst fully onto the scene. 3) Less forgivable as young Lyneker had definitely 'arrived' by the time we played Sheffield Wednesday at Hillsborough in March 1982. 4) Cambridge United away, November 1982. Come on Cambridge... Linneker? you're just taking the piss, everybody has heard of him by now."

If you have any more examples or video footage of Mick Channon trying to pronounce Gary's surname during the 1986 World Cup, then send them to Paul, not us.

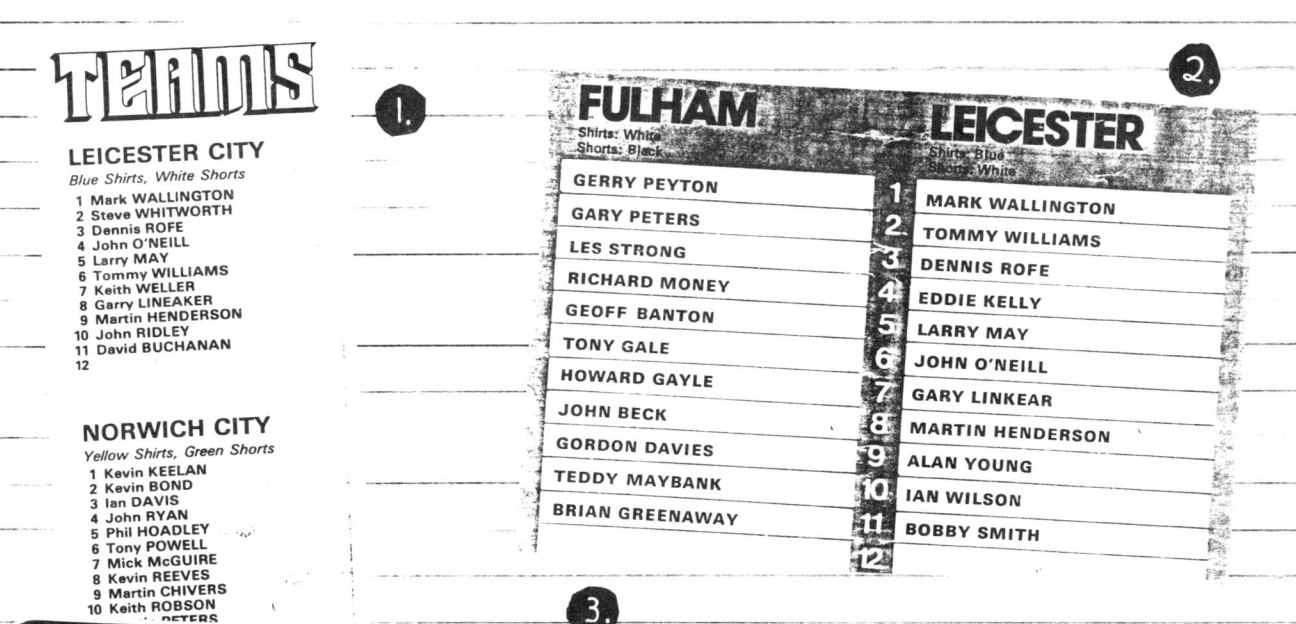

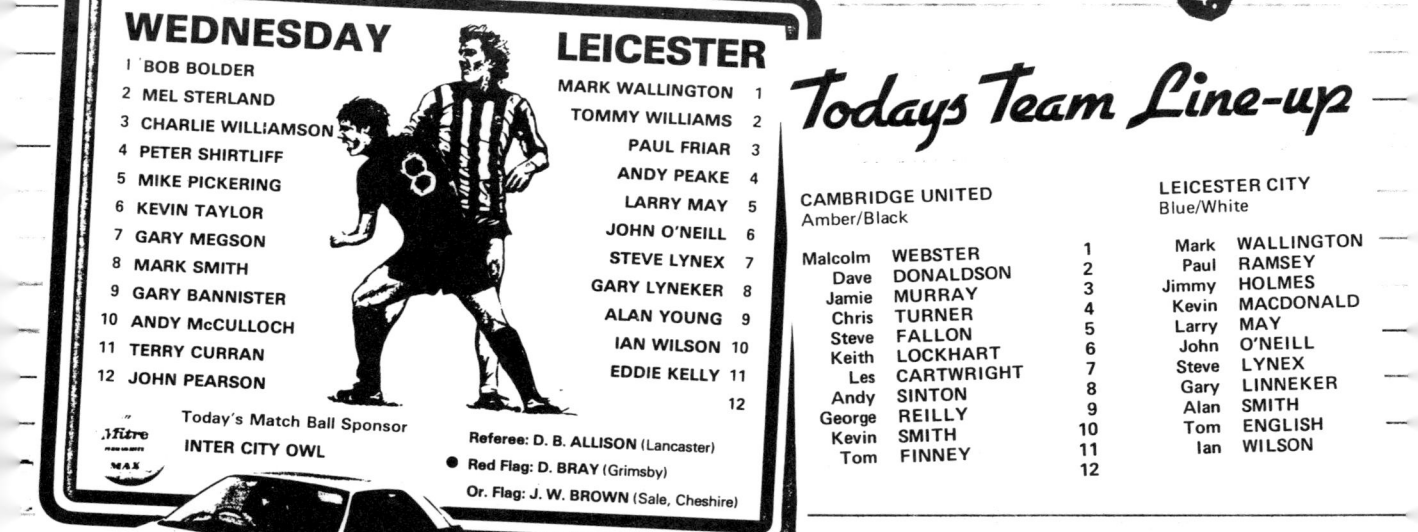

1. TEAMS

LEICESTER CITY
Blue Shirts, White Shorts
1 Mark WALLINGTON
2 Steve WHITWORTH
3 Dennis ROFE
4 John O'NEILL
5 Larry MAY
6 Tommy WILLIAMS
7 Keith WELLER
8 Garry LINEAKER
9 Martin HENDERSON
10 John RIDLEY
11 David BUCHANAN
12

NORWICH CITY
Yellow Shirts, Green Shorts
1 Kevin KEELAN
2 Kevin BOND
3 Ian DAVIS
4 John RYAN
5 Phil HOADLEY
6 Tony POWELL
7 Mick McGUIRE
8 Kevin REEVES
9 Martin CHIVERS
10 Keith ROBSON

2. FULHAM v LEICESTER

FULHAM — Shirts: White, Shorts: Black
1 GERRY PEYTON
2 GARY PETERS
3 LES STRONG
4 RICHARD MONEY
5 GEOFF BANTON
6 TONY GALE
7 HOWARD GAYLE
8 JOHN BECK
9 GORDON DAVIES
10 TEDDY MAYBANK
11 BRIAN GREENAWAY

LEICESTER — Shirts: Blue, Shorts: White
1 MARK WALLINGTON
2 TOMMY WILLIAMS
3 DENNIS ROFE
4 EDDIE KELLY
5 LARRY MAY
6 JOHN O'NEILL
7 GARY LINKEAR
8 MARTIN HENDERSON
9 ALAN YOUNG
10 IAN WILSON
11 BOBBY SMITH

3. WEDNESDAY v LEICESTER

WEDNESDAY
1 BOB BOLDER
2 MEL STERLAND
3 CHARLIE WILLIAMSON
4 PETER SHIRTLIFF
5 MIKE PICKERING
6 KEVIN TAYLOR
7 GARY MEGSON
8 MARK SMITH
9 GARY BANNISTER
10 ANDY McCULLOCH
11 TERRY CURRAN
12 JOHN PEARSON

Today's Match Ball Sponsor
INTER CITY OWL

LEICESTER
1 MARK WALLINGTON
2 TOMMY WILLIAMS
3 PAUL FRIAR
4 ANDY PEAKE
5 LARRY MAY
6 JOHN O'NEILL
7 STEVE LYNEX
8 GARY LYNEKER
9 ALAN YOUNG
10 IAN WILSON
11 EDDIE KELLY
12

Referee: D. B. ALLISON (Lancaster)
Red Flag: D. BRAY (Grimsby)
Or. Flag: J. W. BROWN (Sale, Cheshire)

4. Todays Team Line-up

CAMBRIDGE UNITED — Amber/Black
1 Malcolm WEBSTER
2 Dave DONALDSON
3 Jamie MURRAY
4 Chris TURNER
5 Steve FALLON
6 Keith LOCKHART
7 Les CARTWRIGHT
8 Andy SINTON
9 George REILLY
10 Kevin SMITH
11 Tom FINNEY
12

LEICESTER CITY — Blue/White
1 Mark WALLINGTON
2 Paul RAMSEY
3 Jimmy HOLMES
4 Kevin MACDONALD
5 Larry MAY
6 John O'NEILL
7 Steve LYNEX
8 Gary LINNEKER
9 Alan SMITH
10 Tom ENGLISH
11 Ian WILSON
12

Sunday evening Airfix painting

One Sunday in 1979, during the boring part of the day between 'Last of the Summer Wine' and 'Fawlty Towers', I found myself at a loose end. Too bored to attempt my homework I decided to paint my 1:32nd scale Airfix 'Footballers' set in all the kits that Leicester City had played in during the seventies.... and a bloody good job I made of it too, if that's not blowing my own trumpet (though if I could blow my own trumpet I wouldn't have been bored in the first place). After they were painted each figure spookily took on the guise of a City player: 1970 became Alan Woollett; 1971 was unmistakably David Nish; 1973 looked like John Sjoberg; 1975 was Bob Lee-like; and 1978 looked remarkably like Mark Goodwin. Giving out the orders is Jimmy Bloomfield in his Admiral tracksuit. Painting the red stripes on that tracky top almost sent me blind like Donald Pleasance's master forger in 'The Great Escape'.

1971

1970

1973

1978

1975

Car Boot Sale Shirt Bargains

I found these 1983-84 home and away shirts at a car boot sale. After an 'Antiques Roadshow'-style inspection revealed them to be actual playing strip (fleece-lined, Admiral badges on the numbers, Ind Coope advertising etc.) I opened the bidding.

"How much do you want for these?" I enquired. "Ten Pee..." answered the woman behind the heavily laden decoration table, adding hopefully, "Each".

The Filbert Street Sound

Long playing records, and we don't mean Graham Cross's career stats. These two enormous slabs of vinyl were both pressed in the early 70's but there the similarities end.

'The Best Of Family' LP, sent in by Ian Davidson, is held in high regard among many old heads, and not just because they were such huge City fans that they were known to appear on stage in City shirts as well as on their 'Best Of' cover. Surely the ultimate accolade.

The 'Interview' LP is probably held in high regard by no one. Jon Sammels does a professional enough job on his side, but Shilts gets a bit bogged down over-explaining some of Jeff Astle's 'hilarious' antics while away on England duty... "Jeff was a character, he kept the players in the England squad in stitches, literally in stitches. Players like Alan Ball and Bobby Moore were sort of rolling about with laughter and this takes some doing because these are established players. One of his jokes, which I thought was quite funny, came after we had just finished a tremendously hard training session. The players were shattered and as they were walking back to the coach there was an ITN film crew with Gerald Seymour trying to get interviews with the players. He had a microphone and all that heavy equipment but they didn't want to be bothered with them at that particular moment so they walked past them and onto the coach and sat down and had a drink. Jeff was one of the last players onto the coach and he just stood at the top of the coach and shouted out in his very comic voice: "Having a bad'un, News At Ten, Gerald Seymour, Mexico City"! Er... it was only a very small joke... but the players were in stitches... obviously being thousands of miles from home... er... it was the type of thing that Jeff came out with all the while." Thanks for the warning, Peter.

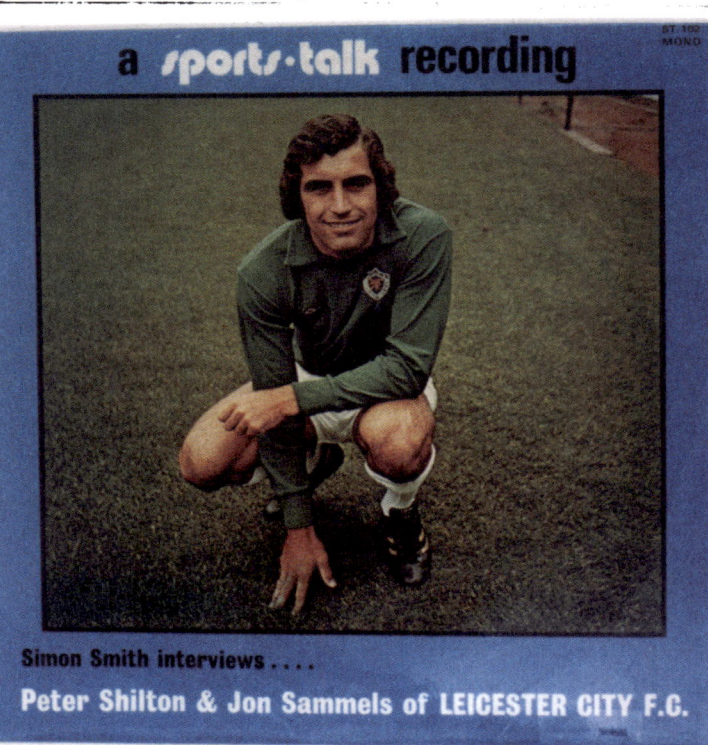

The Garry Parker Gallery

Some players tend to crop up time and time again amongst your Big Blue Scrapbook offerings and Garry Parker is one of them. Luke Bevans sent us this cutting from the Oxford Mail showing a photo of young Garry Parker (front row centre) not to mention young Martin Keown (back row third from left) turning out for Oxfordshire Schools.

"Here's Garry looking like very young captain material", commented Luke, "Not like at City!

Must have been before the beer and pies started kicking in. But I bet he could still do a killer cross-field pass - even at ten..."

Similar weight-related jibes could have been directed towards our midfield maestro following the publication of this highly unflattering 1996-97 'Merlin Premier League Collectors Card'
The player stats on the reverse of the card reckon that Garry is: Height 1.80M, Weight 78KG, but surely they have got those figures the wrong way round?

In July 1996 the 'City Gallery' on Granby Street held a football exhibition called 'The Beautiful Game' as part of the general Euro 96 shin-dig.
My brother John went along for a look and who should be there but City's midfield Generalissimo Garry Parker. One of the exhibits consisted of of large painted board with a hole where you could put your face through and have your photo taken so that it looked as though you were playing in a real professional football match in front of a big crowd.
But, irony of ironies, it was Garry Parker who shoved his face through the hole... and he is *already a professional footballer who plays in front of big crowds!!*

Dean Gale's Great Big City Collection

Dean Gale, arch City stuff collector, has moved back to Australia and taken all his huge mound of Filbo related curios with him. So we couldn't stick any of it in the Big Blue Scrapbook, but he has sent us a photo. Ooo, hasn't it grown?

73

Well, it Looked Alright

Don't listen to those camera snobs who tell you that your happy, crappy, snappy camera isn't suitable for taking football shots... take them anyway! So what if you can't focus on anything, the depth of field is all wrong and the flash is only useful for illuminating the backs of fellow supporter's heads. It's the thought that counts, and who hasn't thought, "Hey, I know! I'm going to take my camera to the game today." Well, now you've had your work published in a book, and that bloke who buys 'Amateur Photographer' hasn't. So there.

A long-range free-kick for City at Anfield in 1981, taken from even longer range by Sue Williamson. City beat Liverpool 2-1.

These two photos of City playing Charlton at The Valley in the early 80's were sent in to The FOX many years ago and became seperated from their owners name, sorry. They do illustrate why the club left this ground though.

Through the Viewfinder

One of my efforts entitled 'A Blue Oasis in a Desert of Red' - City fans in the Scoreboard End Paddock at Old Trafford in 1986. That bloke with the neck tattoo looks hard. We'll walk behind him after the game.

A good City turnout in the Rookery at Vicarage Road in 1992. A microscopic examination of the Watford pen reveals eight Hornet's supporters.

City at The Dell in 1987, before the days of all-seater stadia, a roof over your head, or even a view of the goal for your four quid.

Ian 'Banger' Banks in the same match only seconds later. That stand up the far end will look great when it's finished.

Rob Coe captured both legs of our short UEFA Cup jaunt of 1997 on film. In this photo from the Estadio Vicente Calderon the ants in the white shorts are City.

While in this one the Atletico Madrid players are clearly intimdated whilst warming up beneath the towering edifice of the East Stand.

The Rosette Set

In the olden days males above the age of six could only wear brown, grey, greeny brown, or in moments of extreme flamboyance... navy. It was the Law of England. If you had worn a football jersey when not playing football you would have been arrested. So how to show which set of chaps you were supporting in the big cup game on Saturday? That's where rosettes come in.... and it is no co-incidence that they disappeared when the law changed to allow blokes to wear primary colours. As Sue Williamson's collection, pinned into the Big Blue Scrapbook below, indicates they were especially popular for FA Cup matches. GOOD LUCK LEICESTER!

A Bold Attempt

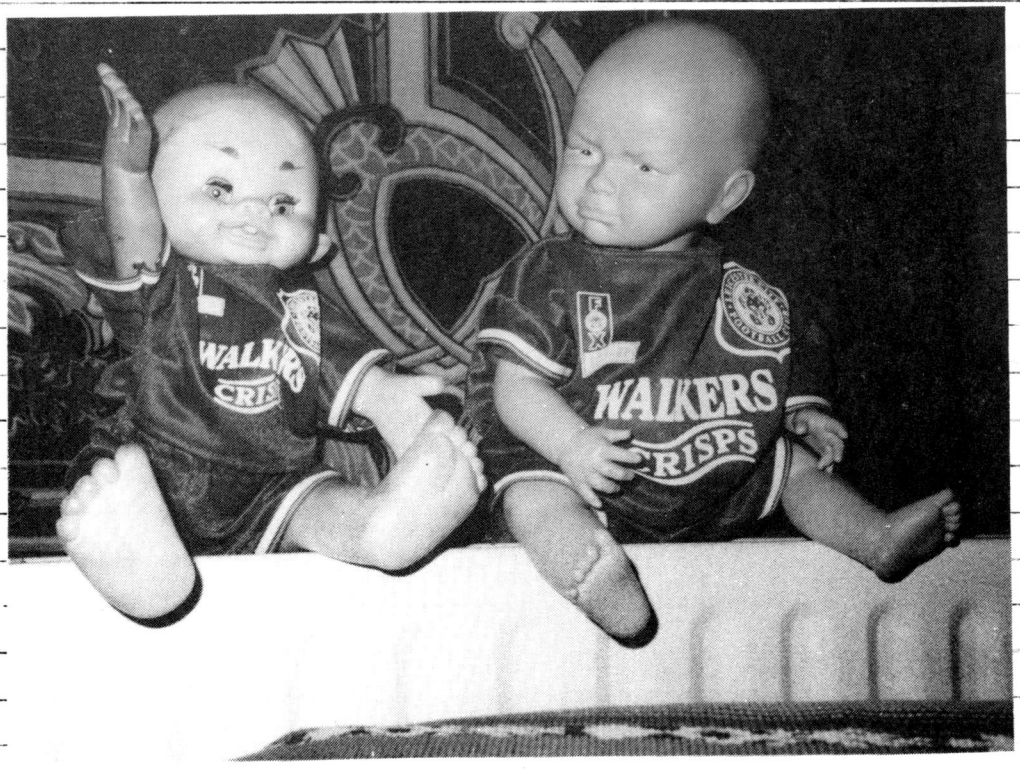

We don't have the name of the person who sent this photo into The FOX several years ago... but we have to say that their models of Steve Agnew (left) and Kevin 'Rooster' Russell really hit the nail on the head. Don't leave them on the radiator for too long though will you?

Tony & Thomas

In the season after Tony James rescued City from the catastrophe of relegation to the Third Division with his 'Great Escape' goal, he broke his leg in a match against dirty Wolves. Here's a photo of Tony recovering at his parent's home in Sheffield. He has his well earned Player of the season Trophy for company, as well as us, a FOX Summer Special 1991 and a huge Thomas the Tank Engine pouffe, which gave him support through his convalescence.

Put the Flags Out

In 1982 these splendid flags appeared in the club shop, the ideal decoration for any blue-blooded City fans' wall. My mate and I both purchased one at the reasonable sum of £1.95 and stuck them onto garden canes liberated from his Dad's garden shed. They made the journey to Crystal Palace for an FA Cup Third Round match in January 1984 and were hung proudly in the windows and held in place by blue and white balloons. Tragedy was to strike... the 'Melton' bus had some lively inhabitants back in those days, and soon after we had entered London's Busy West End one member had decided to cling to the bus ceiling and do a wee out of the skylight. Although it was an impressive trick, to be fair, it has to be said that his aim wasn't too good and one of the flags became liberally splashed with this man's wee. Understandably it was not reclaimed by my mate when we eventually got off the bus. If you look closely there is a sort of sadness about this flag, which is still mourning its partner who suffered such a terrible fate... and some splashback.

We were quietly pleased with the painstakingly put together FOX St George Flag that we took to Sweden for Euro 92... until Kenny from Fleckney arrived. His loving girlfriend had sewn three double bed sheets together to produce a City flag the size of Luxembourg, which dwarfed even the one the Chelsea fans had stolen from a battleship.

The
LEICESTER CITY

Buddens
CC01
1

Buddens
CC01
1
HOLIDAYS & TRAVEL

Canyersignthisfer

The autograph is a funny old thing. Hastily signed... long treasured.

Here is a prime example of a great autograph (right). The signature of World Cup winner Gordon Banks on a photo of himself. That's mine that is.

Below is a prime example of a crap waste of time... the autograph's inferior and pointless cousin, the *photocopied sheet* of players autographs, removing the very personalised point of the signature.

If you wrote off to the club asking for autographs and got one of these back then you were having a 'mare.

On the facing page is a football signed by the Boys of '89 which was booted into the crowd before a Boxing Day fixture against Bournemouth. (It was always Bournemouth wasn't it?).

It was presented to me at my wedding eight years later by Matt Francis, my best man, who had managed to beat off several small children to catch it and always knew that I sort of wanted it. From this angle you can see the scrawls of Ali Mauchlen, Simon Morgan and Marc North. We tried other angles but, believe me, this was the best.

Nigel Noble's dogged determination and teenage lack of any social graces whatever won him this prized autograph back in 1981... Nige explains:

"I was about fifteen, and doing a football pools round (I cannot remember

Gordon Banks O.B.E.

Leicester Autographs

meplease?

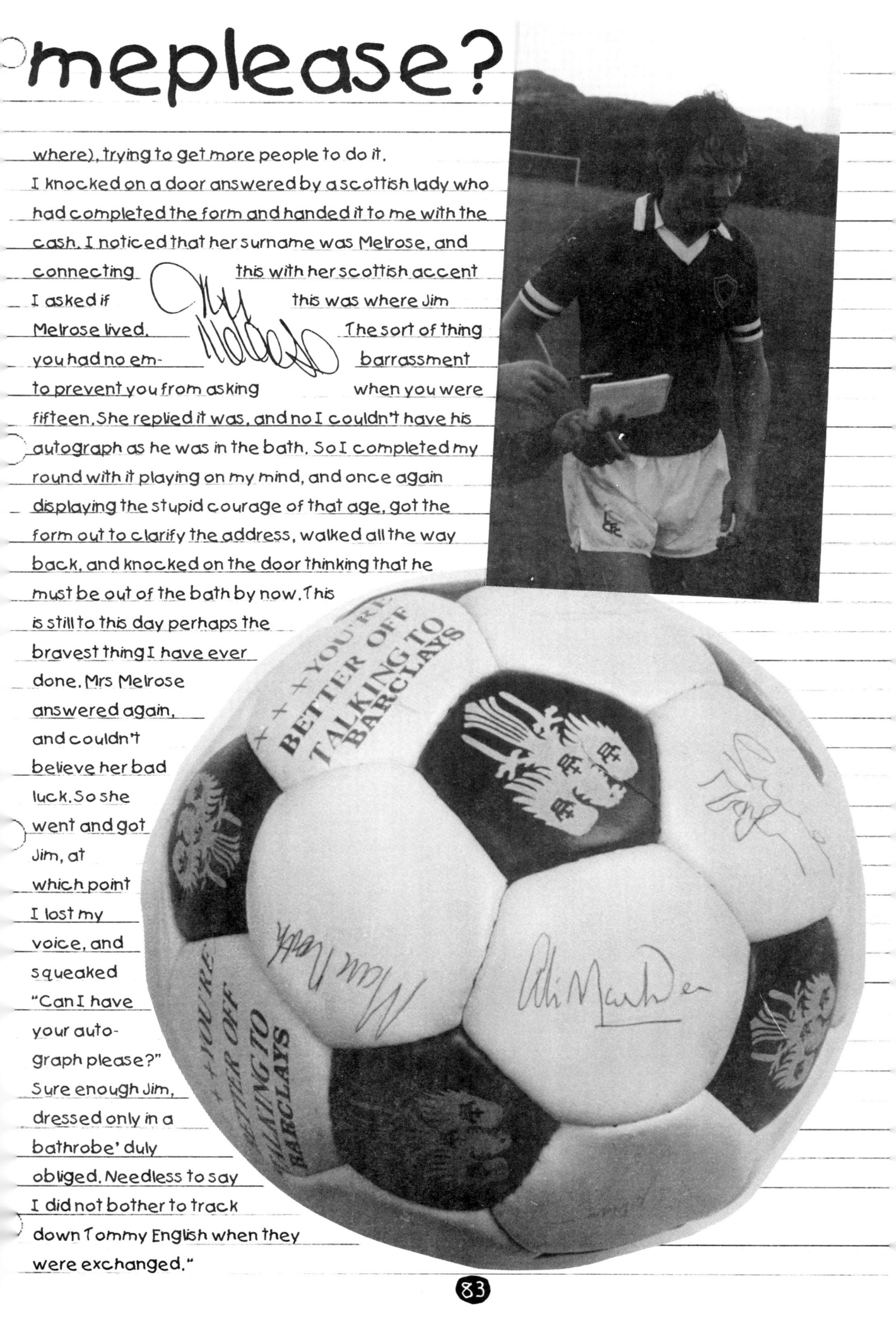

where), trying to get more people to do it. I knocked on a door answered by a scottish lady who had completed the form and handed it to me with the cash. I noticed that her surname was Melrose, and connecting this with her scottish accent I asked if this was where Jim Melrose lived. The sort of thing you had no embarrassment to prevent you from asking when you were fifteen. She replied it was, and no I couldn't have his autograph as he was in the bath. So I completed my round with it playing on my mind, and once again displaying the stupid courage of that age, got the form out to clarify the address, walked all the way back, and knocked on the door thinking that he must be out of the bath by now. This is still to this day perhaps the bravest thing I have ever done. Mrs Melrose answered again, and couldn't believe her bad luck. So she went and got Jim, at which point I lost my voice, and squeaked "Can I have your autograph please?" Sure enough Jim, dressed only in a bathrobe' duly obliged. Needless to say I did not bother to track down Tommy English when they were exchanged."

Sometimes a footballer's autograph can appear in the form of wanton vandalism. Andy Sibson sent this book in to The FOX with the message:

"Please find enclosed a copy of 'A Kind of Loving' by Stan Barstow. A friend of mine owned this book, but was away at university when a certain young Garry Parker was in digs with her mother. Upon her return one vacation she was appalled to find that the apprentice midfield genius had utilised the novel for autograph practise. To compound the felony he had also left himself a couple of notes; namely "MONEY FOR JACKET" on the inside front cover and "PUT LONG STUDS INTO my football Boots. Vital." on page 177. I am sure that the time has come for justice to be done and I commend the book to The FOX in anticipation that someone might wish to donate a sum to charity in return for ownership of the offending material. Come on Garry, time to make amends, or will a fan outbid you for this unique item of memorabilia?"

'And I could apply for a divorce?'
'I should think so.'
'D'you think she would come? She'd have to go out to work again to help pay the rent.'
'Why don't you ask her?'
'How the hell can I?' I say, getting riled again. 'Her mother 'ud go hairless at the thought.'
'I don't want a bald wife,' he says, 'but we'll have to risk it, won't we?'
'You mean . . . ?'
'I mean that what Ingrid's mother thinks in this case is secondary to what Ingrid herself thinks. If you want to see her, then –' He stops. '*Do* you want to see her?'
I wait a minute, then I say, 'I think maybe I should.'
'All right, then. Where?'
'Not at your house.'
This time he does smile, a real smile and no mistake about it.
'Now Ingrid's mother *would* go hairless if I suggested that,' he says.

'Well, that's his fault, isn't it, not mine? If he's daft enough to booze it, it's his lookout, not mine.'
We're walking along side by side and she takes my arm and gives it a squeeze. 'You're a funny lad,' she says.
'Don't I know it,' I say.
A while later we're together in the dark at the back of the picture house and I'm holding her and kissing her and for a while it's nearly like the first time I ever did it. Nearly – but not quite.

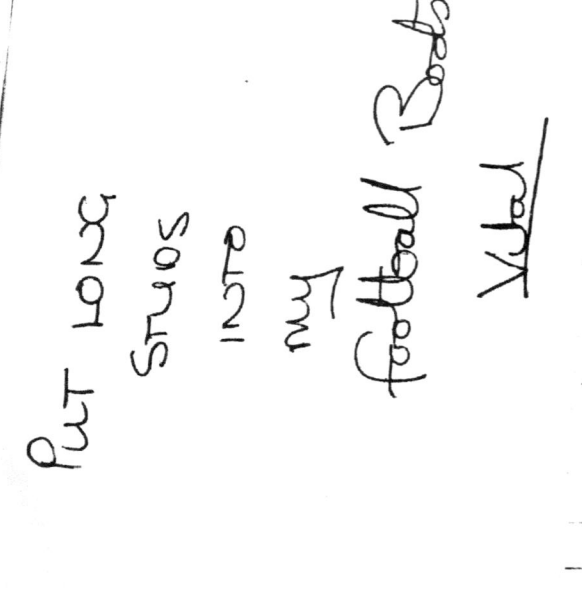

Another way of getting a footballer's autograph is on a business document. As in this example of a Leicester City player whose name shall remain Pontus Kaamark. We received this garage bill with the message: "Leicester can play football!!! *But can they tell petrol from diesel*" written on it. Poor old Pontus had filled his BMW up with the wrong fuel on the way to Wembley for the 1996 Play Off Final. When we asked him about the incident he admitted:

"I have a turbo diesel here in England and I have a lead-free one in Sweden. I filled my turbo diesel with lead-free gas, right up to the top. The car ran for about a mile and then it just died, exactly outside a hotel car park. I don't know anything about cars, but I know that it isn't going to work if it's full of the wrong fuel. It made me late for the game and I had to convince the stewards that I was a Leicester City player, they didn't really believe me!"

An All Time (Har)Low

Yes, it happened... Jock's all-conquering heroes were knocked out of the FA Cup by a team with tickets like this, a wonky typewriter belonging to Phil 'The Prog' Tuson and a goalkeeper called Paul Kitson. And Paul Jackson from Clanfield was there... "In 1980 I had a really bad job, working for a major grocer retailer in North London, and I hated every minute. I was supposed to work on Saturdays, but suffered regular bouts of illness to enable me to watch City instead.

THE OWL REVIEW
Vol. 2 No. 17

FA CUP
THIRD ROUND REPLAY
v. Leicester City
Tuesday 8th. January 1980
Kick-off 7.30 p.m.
Official Programme 20p.

One Saturday, when I was sadly well enough to work, I was sitting in trap 3 in the staff bogs listening to the footy results..... Leicester City 1 Harlow Town 1. After the initial shock it dawned on me that Harlow was somewhere near London and I would be able to go to the replay. The fact that Harlow were little more than a tadpole in

Good evening everyone. Tonight we are delighted to be able to welcome the Players, Officials and Foolowers of Leicester City Football Club. We wish them an enjoyable stay with us, although we can't wish them much luck on the field.

Tonight see's yet another stage in Harlow's sudden rise to fame, with the visit of Leicester City who are currently lying fourth in the Football League Second Division just three points behind leaders Newcastle United. Leicester must have fancied their chances on Saturday having just found their own form with recent home wins over Queens Park Rangers (2-0), and Bristol Rovers (3-0), but on the day it was eleven versus eleven and although being put under tremendous pressure for long periods of the match, we survived and now have home advantage, so we must fancy our chances a little bit.

It was interesting to see that a local bookmaker was offering 4-1 odds against Harlow pulling off another giant killing act. Having said that we fancy our chances tonight, we must come back to earth a little bit and have a look at Leicester's away form this season. Out of a total of eleven away League games they have only lost three, at Newcastle 3-2, Charlton 2-0 and Chelsea 1-0. On the other hand they have only won four, at QPR 4-1, Swansea 2-0, Watford 3-1 and Birmingham 2-1. The rmaining games resulted in draws, against Cambridge 1-1, Shrewsbury 2-2, Oldham 1-1 and finally Preston North End 1-1.

In the Football League Cup Leice ter went out over two legs to Third Division Rotherham United 2-1 at home and 0-3 away.

By tonight we will already know who the winner of tonight's game play, let's keep our fing s crossed that we actually play in the fourth round and that we don't meet Manchester United or Liverpool until the Final.

Keep up the support and see you soon,

Phil (The Prog.) Tuson

the big pond of football, played in a tiny ground, and would sell out of tickets in no time did not occur to me for one moment. Not only that, but a Sheffield Wednesday supporting mate said that he would come along for the ride. On the evening in question it bucketed down with rain and the journey to this New Town in the middle of nowhere in my dodgy VW Polo was a nightmare. We eventually got there, parked up and walked to the joke that they called a ground. No offence Harlow, but it was just a pitch inside a running track with one side being a muddy bank for the City fans to stand on and the other side being a tiny stand which offered the only shelter from the constant pissing rain. Then further misery... the game was all-ticket. We wandered around in hope of finding a couple of spares and were close to giving up and finding a pub when..... BINGO! A City fan offered us two tickets at face value which had been supplied by Bobby Smith. They were ours for £3. Once inside the ground we realised that those priceless bits of paper were for the stand... and not only that but they were in a row directly behind the directors and right in front of me was Andy Peake who was out with an injury. The rest of the stand was full of Harlow fans wearing brand new red and white scarves and bobble hats who probably had as much difficulty finding the ground as we did! The rest, as they say, is history. We lost 1-0. That ticket stayed in my wallet for years afterwards and is now normally housed in a little frame on my toilet wall. Why? Well why not? I bet no one else has got one! I have never been to Harlow since, and I never will..."

F.A. CUP

HARLOW TOWN
v
LEICESTER CITY

TUES. 8th JANUARY 1980   K.O. 7.30

ADMIT ONE
SEATING   No   006
£3.00

F.A. CUP

HARLOW HUMBLE CITY

by Bill Anderson

AN INCREDIBLE second half slump by Leicester City cost them any chance of replying to the first half goal that gave Isthmian League side Harlow Town a 1-0 win in last night's FA Cup third round replay at the Harlow Sports Centre.

After a passable first-half display when they had the bulk of play, and chances, City crumbled to the level of their surroundings, unaccountably electing to play the non-league side at their own game. What got in to the City players then, I'll never know.

Time and again they used the last refuge of the unimaginative — a high punt up the middle. All this did was to flatten the heads of the Harlow defenders. They might not have been able to deal with City's work on the ground but the high stuff was easy meat.

Even then, four clear-cut chances, two each to Martin Henderson and Alan Young, were thrown away because, at that stage, midway through the second half, City had lost their nerve and couldn't put together even the simplest move.

What made it all so unbelievable as the game drew to its inevitable conclusion was that City, as they had shown in the first half, had the beating of Harlow if they had stuck to their task. The pattern of the first match at Filbert Street was soon set.

Gary Lineker stretched the home defence and, in an incredible period of fierce pressure, Harlow 'keeper Paul Kitson tipped over headers from Young and Henderson and a shot by O'Neill as City forced four corners in a row.

Scrappy goal

Although City had eight corners to Harlow's one in the first half it was then that the match-winning goal was scored in the 42nd minute. It was a scrappy effort but, in the final analysis it was the most golden goal of this or any other month as far as Harlow is concerned.

A swerving free-kick was deflected off Larry May and Neil Prosser to John Mackenzie who turned the ball towards goal in the scramble. Tommy Williams hacked it clear but the ball it did not, and you could sense the home club making sure from that point that there was plenty of champagne to go round.

It was the turning point of the game. All Jock Wallace's principles of fighting spirit, character and concentration on passing went by the board.

Disaster

I think that was more upsetting for him and the City faithful, huddled on the grassy slopes around the ground, than the actual result, which was a disaster.

One significant sidelight of the evening was that Watford manager Graham Taylor and general manager Bertie Mee left the game with 20 minutes left, no doubt feeling they had little or nothing to fear in the next round from either side.

That just about summed up City's performance, and I am sure a lot of their following would have liked to have done the same. Certainly, out on the pitch several City players seemed to have long since given up the ghost.

And that reaction, whether or not the breaks are going against you, is something Wallace will not forgive. After the match, he was at the lowest I've ever seen him after a defeat.

FOILED AGAIN . . . Martin Henderson rushes in to a cross from Alan Young on the right but Kitson makes a diving interception. BELOW: Larry May, up with the City attack, manages to get in a side-foot shot at goal despite close attendance from the Harlow defenders.

Sue Williamson's Car Park Collection

Henderson, Young & page 3 of The Sun...

Bobby Smith's Lovely Motah

Hang around the Filbert Street car park for long enough and you will always find something worth pointing a camera at. Martin and Alan being laddish... Bobby proudly showing off his fine new sponsored Yugo from Barwell.... Gary trying out some new fashion ideas... or young David being hugged by a someone who we suspect might be a Scandanavian...'Have you got any Viking in you?' All human life can be found beneath the big pylon...

Garry Linykarr - style guru

Dave Buchannan and an admirer

and then sneaking up the tunnel...

It's no good, she just can't resist it. Not content with all the crazy car park activity, as soon as the dozy receptionist has nodded off Sue is through the main entrance, down the tunnel and out onto the pitch surround in the flash of an eye. And what does she find within Filbert Street's hallowed inner sanctum? Wise old captain Eddie Kelly and big bluff manager Jock Wallace going for a lovely walk in the last warm rays of the evening sunshine. And look there's that lovely fella Mark Wallington who has just finished doing some weeding in the Filbert Street End goalmouth.

What an idyllic English pastoral scene.......... quick Sue, LEG IT! Here comes the groundsman and his pit bull....

Fan the Flames

City supporters being actively pissed off with the club did not begin with 'Blue Tuesday' or 'Ambitious Leicester Fans'. This flyer, distributed in 1976 and kept by Sue Williamson, rather blows apart the golden image of Jimmy Bloomfield's legendary seventies side. Does anyone else remember 'BLOOMFIELD OUT!' being written on a hoarding in large blue letters near the Odeon cinema? I wonder what they thought of Frank McLintock the following season?!

Are YOU satisfied with Jimmy Bloomfield's performance as Manager?
Just consider the Facts:-

* Five seasons without success despite over £1m being spent on new players

* Entertainment value could not be lower

* Dissatisfaction amongst the players - Worthington's early season outburst and Garland's sudden departure

* Money available for new players but no attempt to strengthen the side

* Weak excuses given adopting a pathetic patronising attitude towards the fans.

THERE IS NO LONGER ANY PRIDE IN BEING A LEICESTER SUPPORTER

BLOOMFIELD MUST GO

If you agree write to the local press and express your views.

> TO LEICESTER PLAYERS AND FANS.
>
> WELCOME. HAVE A GOOD DAY. MAY THE BETTER TEAM WIN.
>
> TO DERBY FANS
> THE CHANT IS
> CLOUGH IN - BOARD OUT!
> CLOUGHIE SHOUTED FOR YOU
> NOW YOU SHOUT FOR HIM.
> WE WILL WIN!!
>
> *[signed Peter Shilton]*
>
> Short supply Please pass on.
>
> DON SHAW
> BILL HOLMES

Ian Davidson had this grubby leaflet shoved at him before a game at the Baseball Ground in the 1973-74 season. It came about by the miracle reproductive process of what I believe used to be called 'photostat', and was badly handwritten by Derby fans protesting about Brian Clough's departure. Although it is written in 'sheepshagger' we have put some of our best minds on the job and they have come up with the following translation:

"TO LEICESTER PLAYERS AND FANS, WELCOME, HAVE A GOOD DAY, MAY THE BETTER TEAM WIN. TO DERBY FANS, THE CHANT IS 'CLOUGH IN - BOARD OUT!' CLOUGHIE SHOUTED FOR YOU, NOW YOU SHOUT FOR HIM, WE WILL WIN!! SHORT SUPPLY PLEASE PASS ON.
                                        DON SHAW, BILL HOLMES."

Being a loyal City fan and not giving two hoots about Derby's plight Ian did not 'pass on' due to 'short supply'. He got Peter Shilton to autograph it and kept it. Ha!

WE, THE UNDERSIGNED, DISMAYED AT RECENT NEWSPAPER REPORTS, WISH THE CHAIRMAN AND DIRECTORS OF LEICESTER CITY FOOTBALL CLUB TO RECOGNISE THE STRENGTH OF FEELING OF THE CLUB'S SUPPORTERS BY IMMEDIATELY REVERSING THEIR DECISION TO GRANT THE TRANSFER REQUEST SUBMITTED BY MR. KEITH WELLER AND TO GIVE SERIOUS CONSIDERATION TO PROVIDING TERMS AND CONDITIONS OF EMPLOYMENT ACCEPTABLE TO THIS PLAYER.

[Signatures of supporters follow, including: M.D. Rowe, B. Shaw, S. Botherton, C. Haywood, Alison Smith, C. Hibbert, E.M. Farmer, N.J. Farmer, Miss K. Eley, Miss B. McAdam, J. Poulter, D.R. Bradbury, A. Stubbs, G. Featherstone, P. Sellears, S.I. Iuaniece, J. Berwick, E. Berwick, C. Sprigate, F. Cannon, S. Cropper, S. Judge, M. Bliss, J. Drysdale, S.T. Browne, A. Dixon, J.E. Lane, P. Ashore, H. Moore, K. Shaw, Jim Hubbard, Paul Whitlock, Keith Faulkes, K. Dalton, K. Welch, G. Thomson, J. Blockley, D. Davidson, Robert Martain, James D'O, K.A. Moore, G. Brighton, I. Smith, M. Murray, M. Greaves, K. Orr, N. Markham, S. Markham, D. Greaves, A. Sharp, L. Foley, P. Rogers, P. McCartney, D. Elliott, S. Riley, E. Henry, C.D. Smith, Andy Jones, Phil Augustus, A. Cattermole, M. Willbond, R. Deakill, C. Corcoran, J. Prendergast, D. Phillips, S. Burton, S. Verity, O. Bracey, P. Starmer, N. Ashton, K. Soulsby, H. Harper, D. Lee, and others]

The historical document above is part of the 'Keith Weller Petition' instigated by Arthur Hubbard in 1978 when it looked as though Keith Weller might be on his way out of Filbert Street. We might be wrong but we don't think that 'J Blockley' or 'P McCartney' were treating this matter with quite the seriousness it warranted. Unfortunately, as you can see from the Mercury clipping opposite, Arthur's campaign was doomed to failure, with the Filbert Street legend leaving for the New England Tea Men on 1st February 1979, but at least he gave it a bloody good go.

22-11-78

Stay on Keith, say 4,000 fans

FIFTEEN minutes before the kick-off of tonight's match between Leicester City and Wrexham at Filbert Street (7.45), a petition regarding the club's decision to transfer-list Keith Weller will be handed in to the directors' box by organiser Mr. Arthur Hubbard.

And I understand that the number of names on the petition is not far off the 4,000; on current attendances about a third of the crowd. Mr. Hubbard himself is pleased with the response and feels it justifies his personal standpoint.

But he told me: "This is nothing against Jock Wallace. We feel Keith has been hard done by as far as the club is concerned and it will show the directors that the fans will not take this sort of thing lying down.

"The aim is to make the club think in terms of compromise for this season so that we shall be able to see Weller in the side, guiding on the young players that come in."

---

44 LEICESTER MERCURY, THURSDAY, FEBRUARY 1, 1979

WELLER'S FAREWELL

Seven-year-itch leaves City star feeling glum

by Bill Anderson

KEITH WELLER has played his last game for Leicester City. He has been transferred to American club New England Tea Men permanently for the £40,000 fee City manager Jock Wallace had steadfastly demanded.

Although Weller's days at City were clearly numbered on the arrival of Jock Wallace — who was against players being loaned to America and was committed to building up a young team — the final break with the club has still come as a blow to the fans. And also to the player himself.

This morning, as he turned up to do some training with players who were no longer team mates at the ground which is suddenly no longer "home", he told me: "I know I asked for a transfer and that a move has been on the cards for a while but now that it has actually happened I feel a bit numb.

"I've had my ups and downs here, more good times than bad, but I have a special feeling for the place and right at this moment I feel a bit sad to be leaving after seven years.

"The break with City has, after all this time, come a bit sudden and I would dearly have liked to have played one last game in front of the fans who have been so good to me. The 1-1 draw with Blackburn will go down as my last game now.

"It wasn't the high note I wanted to leave on. I didn't play very well myself, and I would have preferred another chance to make my farewell a proper one, although I understand the manager's point of view that once the deal was complete then there was no point in hanging on."

Vindicated

Late last night, the player negotiated with New England manager Noel Cantwell and one of the team's owners Arthur Smith. They had already agreed on the £40,000 price tag which New England and Weller had initially thought was too high.

The fact that three clubs, New England, Chelsea and Seattle Sounders, were all prepared to pay that price vindicates Wallace's standpoint and the City manager is happy with the deal while understanding the depth of feeling for Weller locally.

He said: "After the player's transfer request was granted, three clubs were willing to meet the asking price and the player was allowed to negotiate his own terms with whichever one he chose.

"He had played in America before and was keen to return. I wish him all the best with his new club and hope he is successful."

Wallace had previously said that Weller would not be leaving until after City's fourth round F.A. Cup tie with Oldham. The original game was postponed, being rescheduled for Monday at Boundary Park, and I understand the feeling was that once the New England deal was signed and sealed then that was it all over.

Controversy

Keith Weller's career at City scaled the heights when his brilliant form gained him four England caps in 1974, but the new season the then City skipper was surrounded by controversy when he asked for a transfer and the now-famous incident when he refused to come out for the second half of a home match against Ipswich.

But the real factor governing his future at City was the injury to his right knee in an accidental clash with Steve Whitworth during a home match against Middlesbrough back in March, 1977.

Keith has been the first to admit he could never get back to his former brilliance, but the abiding feeling of the fans was that a half-fit Weller was better than some others in the side.

Their worst fears have now come to fruition. Weller's days at City are over and it is now up to the fans to decide whether they will live in the past and hark back to Weller's brilliance, or support the new team Wallace is building with his Filbert Street youngsters.

A shock for sad Arthur

THE news of Keith Weller's transfer came as a bitter blow to the organiser of the "Keep Keith" campaign, Mr. Arthur Hubbard, because he was all set to see City manager Jock Wallace next Wednesday for a last-resort meeting.

He said today: "This has come as a tremendous shock to me after all the work I had done to try to put forward the case of so many City fans who wanted Keith to stay at Filbert Street.

"We were under no illusions that Keith couldn't last for ever, but the thousands of people who signed my petition showed the strength of feeling on this matter.

"I had arranged to see Jock Wallace next Wednesday to see if there was any way of keeping Keith until the end of the season at least and although the transfer has now gone through, I am still going to have that meeting.

"All along there has never been any quarrel with Mr. Wallace as we appreciate his policy of building up a young side, but so many fans still wanted to see Keith Weller in action a little longer.

"The matter has now been settled, but at least the fans have seen how hard I, and others, have worked to keep Keith at City. We've failed, but I would just like to say that I wish Keith all the very best in America and we will continue to support the new City side."

KEITH WELLER says goodbye to some of his Leicester team mates at Belvoir Drive this morning. From left to right: Steve Whitworth, Dennis Rofe and Mark Wallington.

DON'T
MAR

𝕷eicester 𝕸ercury   𝕷eicest

The 'Don't Go Martin!' Mercury freebie from a night in October 1998 when O'Neill was persuaded that his future lay at Filbert Street. Possibly the Mercury's greatest ever poster campaign, eclipsing even their, 'Little Liar' and 'McGhee is a Fat Judas' efforts.

T GO TIN!

rcury

Wait a Minute Mr Postman

Did you ever have the urge to write to a football club? Did you ever get a reply? If you did was it much, much shorter than your original letter? Pasted into the Big Blue Scrapbook here are:

A) A reply from Jock Wallace to Rob Coe who sent a 'Get Well Soon' card to the City boss while he was in hospital having a knee operation.

B) A note from Rustie Lee's manager replying to a letter in The FOX which showed a photo of the TV cook with a Wolves flag... don't forget that useful mathematical equation: Rustie Lee = Blue Army.

C) A letter to Simon Kimber from Graham Taylor after some City fans were ambushed

---

Leicester City Football Club Co. Ltd.

Registered Office: CITY STADIUM, FILBERT STREET, LEICESTER, ENGLAND.
Tel. 555000 Telegrams: "Football, Leicester" Company Registration No. 157760

6 November 1980

Master R Coe
Park Road
Earl Shilton
Leicestershire

Dear Robert,

Thank you very much indeed for the good wishes contained in the card that you sent to me recently. The thought is certainly appreciated.

Yours sincerely,

Jock Wallace
Manager

A.

---

irm management

UNIT 45 HARRIERS TRADE CENTRE, STADIUM CLOSE, KIDDERMINSTER, ENGLAND, DY10 1NJ. PHONE (0)1562 820018 · FAX (0)1562 820019

The Editor
The Fox
PO Box 2
Cosby
Leicester
LE9 1ZZ

23.09.1996

Dear Editor,

Rustie Lee & Your reader Paul Tompkins Letter in issue No 62

I do not normally take time out to comment on every article I read in Newspapers or Magazines with regards to Rustie Lee, but this one I thought needed addressing.

Rest assured Paul, Rustie has not and never will desert Leicester City Football Club (It's a matter of the Heart, isn't it?).

The Photograph they've used was taken as part of Central Televisions PR Campaign for Rustie's Television Programme "Rustie's Real Cooks" in which they've featured Wolves as part of one episode. Rustie and myself tried hard to get this Programme filmed with Leicester City Football Club, but at the time the Club had enough on their plate and Central had to use another Midland Club for the Programme. Sensible as TV People are, they've chose Wolves, what can you say?

As for Wolves (or was it for the old wind up merchant MC Ghee) they must be pretty desperate for good publicity.

So Paul and all you Foxes Supporters, here it is once again : Rustie Lee = Blue Army, and should we get the chance to play Wolves during this or any other season (although it can only be in a cup competition), there will be nobody shouting louder for our team then Rustie.

Kind regards,

Andreas Hohmann
irm management

B.

Watford

GT/NW   14th May, 1982.

Mr. S. Kimber,
38, Carlson Gardens,
Lutterworth,
Leics., LE17 4DP.

Dear Simon,

Thank you for your recent letter. I am very much disturbed to hear about the incidents in the town centre after the game against Leicester, and I have forwarded on your comments to the police.

Yours sincerely,

Graham Taylor
Graham Taylor.

C.

D.

Members of the Football League
Division IV Promotion 1959/60
Division III Champions 1968/69
F.A. Cup Semi-Finalists 1969/70
Division IV Champions 1977/78
F.L. Cup Semi-Finalists 1978/79

Leicester City Football Club Co. Ltd

Registered Office: CITY STADIUM, FILBERT STREET, LEICESTER LE2 7FL, ENGLAND
Telephone (0533) 555000 Fax (0533) 470585   Company Registration No. 157760 V.A.T. Registration No. 114 1482 09

Our Ref. MFG/JP

20th March, 1992.

S. Smith Esq.,
20, Overton Drive,
Lea Park,
Thame,
Oxon OX9 3YJ

Dear Mr. Smith,

Thank you for your letter and for taking the trouble to write.

The transfer of Kitson, unlike those of Lineker, Smith and McAllister was completed because Brian Little felt it was in the Club's best interests whereas the others had to be sold to balance our bank account.

There is no doubt in my mind that the changes we have just made, and there may be more before the deadline, have given us a realistic opportunity of achieving a play-off place, which was clearly beyond us without some transfer movement. We also now have additional sums to invest in the summer.

Keep up your support.

Yours sincerely,

Martin George

MARTIN F. GEORGE
Chairman

---

by Watford hooligans. Perhaps it was Dougie and Eddie Violence, the authors. D) Martin George tries to explain himself in the face of Simon Smith's broadside after Paul Kitson was sold. "Yeah, like we're going to make the play-offs now!"

Dave's faves...

We asked FOX photographer Dave Morcom for a selection of his favourite photos taken in eight years of City-related snappery. This is what he came up with...

1) Ian Ormondroyd, always an interesting subject, having a good rummage around in his shorts before a corner against Barnsley. It was usually quite difficult to get Sticks' head and feet in the same shot.

2) Brian Little always looked very uncomfortable whenever we asked him to do something for a shot, but the end results were always quite good. What a pro.

3) Tommy Wright, outside his house in Melton. I know we promised never to print this Tommy, but we lied. Like you did about not leaving City. Although the 'For Sale' sign was a bit of a giveaway, thinking about it.

4) The most requested FOX photo of all time, for some reason. I think we had to print it about three times on the letters page, you dirty monkeys.

5) The celebrations following Richard Smith's late winner against Crystal Palace in the FA Cup... it has a touch of the Crucifixtion about it. I always thought it would make a good statue near the Clocktower.

1.

2.

3.

William H. Brown
RESIDENTIAL
For Sale
Melton Mowbray
(0664) 63481

99

4.

5.

100

Yer Man as a Boy

AS YOU WERE

IN 1971 the 19-year-old Martin O'Neill (left) left Derry City for Nottingham Forest, where he became an integral part of Brian Clough's side that won the First Division title in 1978 and the European Cup in 1979 and 1980 (above). He played 285 times for Forest, and scored 48 goals, as well as gaining 64 international caps for Northern Ireland. In December 1995, via playing spells at a host of clubs and managerial jobs in places as varied as Grantham Town, Shepshed Charterhouse and Wycombe Wanderers, he took over at Leicester, where he remains, if no longer so fresh-faced (right).

Ian Chester carefully snipped this piece out of the Independent and sent it in to us. "Here's great picture of O'God in his younger days", says Ian. "Though I'm not too sure what that air hostess has just discovered nestling in Martin's breast pocket. He looks quite guilty though. I hope I won't be held responsible for introducing a Forest badge into the Big Blue Scrapbook if you use it." Don't worry Ian, we aren't too concerned with that Nationwide outfit. They won't be winning any more European Cups in the near future.

Alien Invasion

...1968...1968...1968...1968...1968...
LEICESTER CITY FANS

L.C.F.C. LEICESTER CITY FOOTBALL CLUB

"Come along now, chaps — cough up. We need a ball!"

Like so many famous clubs, LEICESTER CITY started in a very humble way. In 1884 some old boys of Wyggeston School subscribed 7½d each to form a club which they called LEICESTER FOSSE. "The Fossils" made progress and in 1894 were elected to the Second Division of the League.

The club's name was changed to Leicester City in 1919. Always a good club with many fine players, but never a great one where honours are concerned, City have never won the championship — although they missed the title in 1928-29 by just a solitary point. They have also topped Division Two four times — 1925, 1937, 1954 and 1957.

Among their stars of the period between the wars were ARTHUR CHANDLER (above), leading scorer with 291 League goals, and little wing-wizard HUGHIE ADCOCK, who played in 434 games for City. Both played for England.

Chandler's club record of 33 goals in a season (1925) was smashed in 1957 by ARTHUR ROWLEY, who reached a total of 44 goals. Arthur, now manager of Shrewsbury, scored 251 goals during his career with Leicester City.

Rowley never played for England, but two of their 1957 promotion side did — centre-half JACK FROGGATT (top) and inside-forward JOHNNY MORRIS.

City have reached the F.A. Cup Final three times since the war, but have been losers on every occasion. However, they did win the Football League Cup in 1964.

Of more recent years, Leicester teams have included several famous players: COLIN APPLETON (left) was their skipper in two finals (1961 and 1963) and is now player-manager at Barrow. FRANK McLINTOCK, a Scottish International, is now captain of Arsenal.

GORDON BANKS, England's goalie in so many internationals and a star of the World Cup winning team, is now with Stoke City.

MATT GILLIES, a Scot who joined City as a centre-half in 1952, has been their manager since 1958.

26

102

Tiger & Scorcher say: "Okay, we know that some of these players might look like alien beings who have been placed among us to take over human society from the inside, but......... Leicester City Fans - This is Your Team! Honest."

THIS IS YOUR TEAM!

TODAY'S STARS

EARLIER THIS SEASON CITY SIGNED THREE EXPENSIVE STARS. **WILLIE BELL** IS A STOCKY SCOTTISH DEFENDER, SIGNED FROM LEEDS UNITED. HE HAD BEEN AT ELLAND ROAD FOR SEVEN YEARS.

FRANK LARGE IS A TALL, HEFTY, GOALSCORING FORWARD, COMING FROM NORTHAMPTON TOWN. A SPLENDID BUY FOR CITY, HE HAS ALSO PLAYED FOR SWINDON, CARLISLE AND OLDHAM.

LEN GLOVER IS A FLEET-FOOTED, SHARPSHOOTING WINGER WHO COST CITY £80,000 FROM CHARLTON.

PETER RODRIGUES IS A BRILLIANT WELSH INTERNATIONAL FULL-BACK, FORMERLY WITH CARDIFF CITY.

LEICESTER WERE ABLE TO TRANSFER GORDON BANKS FOR A FEE OF £52,000 (IN APRIL 1967) BECAUSE HIS UNDERSTUDY WAS **PETER SHILTON**, ONE OF THE GREATEST GOALKEEPING PROSPECTS IN THE GAME. A LOCAL LAD, HE WAS A STAR OF ENGLAND'S SCHOOLBOY TEAMS OF 1965.

MIKE STRINGFELLOW IS A TALL, WILLOWY CENTRE-FORWARD AND A FORMER WINGER. HE COST LEICESTER £25,000 FROM MANSFIELD TOWN IN 1962.

JOHN SJOBERG, CITY'S CAPTAIN AND CENTRE-HALF, BORN IN ABERDEEN, WAS A SCOTTISH SCHOOLBOY INTERNATIONAL IN 1958 AND JOINED THE LEICESTER STAFF IN 1958.

RITCHIE NORMAN, LEFT-BACK IN LEICESTER'S TWO CUP FINAL SIDES, IS ONE OF THE CLUB'S LONGEST-SERVING PLAYERS. HE JOINED THEM IN 1955 FROM HORDEN COLLIERY, NEAR HIS NATIVE NEWCASTLE.

ANOTHER £25,000 SIGNING, FROM HIBS, IS **DAVIE GIBSON**. A TRADITIONAL SCOTTISH-TYPE INSIDE-FORWARD, "WEE DAVIE" IS A SCOTTISH INTERNATIONAL, TOO.

27

Cheryl Boulton's

In best 'Tiger & Scorcher' or 'Shoot & Goal' tradition it is time for the Big Blue Scrapbook to incorporate Cheryl Boulton's Medium Sized Blue Photo Album. It's chock full of all your favourite City Stars from recent history.... A) Cheryl on a big night out with some footballers... and Lee Philpott. B) Cheryl and her favourite, Stevie Claridge, just before he sets off for the bookies, allegedly. Probably. C) Stars in Their Cars... keep your eyes on the road Spencer, you

A.

B.

104

Photo Frenzy...

know what happened last time. D) Super Stevie again, on the way back from the bookies. See overleaf E) F) & G) Cheryl meets Robbie, Emile and Tony at sunny Belvoir Drive....
H) Mighty Matt Elliott shows Cheryl how big and tough he is by lifting two small weights.
I) Oo look, it's that bloke off the telly... Garry Lynnekker. and finally J) What better way to bring the Big Blue Scrapbook to a close than by sticking in this last photo of Cheryl and Martin? Goodbye, I'm so very tired...

E.

F.

G.

H.

I.

J.

107

The End

Thanks...

Grateful thanks go to everyone who sent stuff in or helped in any way with the Big Blue Scrapbook:
Luke Bevans, Andy Buckingham, Tim Burke, Ian Chester, Rob Coe, Ian Davidson, Matt Francis, Dean Gale, Geoff Scott's Aunty?, Dave Goodacre, Paul Henderson, Chris Horner, Helen Hyatt, Mick Iwaszko, Paul Jackson, Jurgen, Jon Knighton, Peter Mays, Dave Morcom, Nigel Noble, Clive Payne, Farley Pig, Sue Riley, Andy Sibson, Joan Sibson, John Silke, Simon Smith, Steve the Nottingham Blue, Leo Tennant, Matt Warrington, Richard West and extra special thanks to Sue Williamson without whom this book would have been half the size.

Subscriptions...

You probably already know this but The Big Blue Scrapbook appears monthly in the Leicester City Fanzine 'THE FOX', the monthly fix of City-related news, views, humour and nostalgia...

To receive 'The FOX Summer Special 1999' and each monthly issue of the 1999-2000 season send a cheque for £12.70, payable to 'The FOX' to:

PO BOX No 2, Cosby, Leicester, LE9 1ZZ.

Other interesting football books from

Juma
PRINTERS, PUBLISHERS, BOOKSELLERS

IF THE REDS SHOULD PLAY...
Travelling Across Europe With Manchester United
edited by Barney Chilton, Martin Day, Phil Holt & Phil Williams
200pp A5 paperback ISBN 1 872204 45 7
£7.99 (+ £1.25 p&p/Europe £2.50/ Rest £5)
Twenty chapters from twenty writers, including former United player Arthur Albiston, the editors of United fanzines Red News and United We Stand, terrace songsmith Pete Boyle and Adam Brown from the FSA, each giving their personal account of a memorable trip to a United away game in Europe over the past twenty years. Triumphs and humiliations, the fun and the frightening, the drunken and the bizarre. True stories describing what travelling to a football match abroad is really like.

WE ARE WOLVES
Wolverhampton Wanderers - The Fans Story
edited by Charles Ross
200pp sub-A4 paperback ISBN 1 872204 35 X
£9.95 (+£1.50 p&p/Europe £3/ Rest £6)
In the fans' own words, the special appeal of a club that has spent nearly forty years trying to recapture the glory days of the 50s, when the team of Stan Cullis and Billy Wright turned Wolverhampton Wanderers into Europe's finest. This is the story of rollercoaster ride since that golden post-war era. Nostalgia: from charting the fortunes of the team and a young follower in the 60s to rites of passage tales from the 70s and 80s. Hero worship: of two great strikers, John Richards and Steve Bull. Despair: as Wolves' decline in the 80s took them to the Fourth Division and to the brink of extinction. Delight: as Wolves climbed out of the abyss with two successive promotions. Frustration: of the wilderness years of Division One and the heartache of two play-off defeats. Over twenty authors from the A Load Of Bull fanzine provide a rivetting insight into what Wolves mean to them.

PINNACLE OF THE PERRY BARR PETS
The Men And Matches Behind Aston Villa's 1897 Double
by Simon Page
102pp sub-A4 paperback ISBN 1 872204 30 9
£6.95(+ £1 p&p/ Europe £2/ Rest £4)
1897: Aston Villa complete the League Chapionship and FA Cup Double. 1997: The true and complete story of the men and matches that made history is finally recorded in a single volume. Pinnacle Of The Perry Barr Pets details every match played by Villa's finest ever line-up during the club's most successful season ever. An exhilarating journey through the last days of the Wellington Road ground, via Crystal Palace and arguably the greatest Cup Final of all time, to the opening of Villa Park, then the best stadium in the World. Includes biographies of all the players and major backroom staff and offers a unique insight into the running of a 19th Century footballing giant, aswell as the lives of footballers before the days of multi-million pound signings, extortionate wages and television.

GLADYS PROTHEROE... FOOTBALL GENIUS!
by Simon Cheetham with foreword by Graham Taylor
220pp A5 paperback ISBN 1 872204 10 4
£5.95 (+£1.25 p&p/Europe £2.50/Rest £5)
From the sun-baked terraces of the Maracana to the frozen teahut at Vicarage Road, supporters throughout the world love and respect Gladys Protheroe. Who discovered John Barnes (and Bruce Springsteen)? Who persuaded Alf Ramsey that Geoff Hurst was a better prospect than Jimmy Greaves? Who punched Ron Atkinson on live TV? And the astonishing truth behind Stuart Pearce's suicidal back pass against San Marino. Over half a century of football history and - sometimes shocking - revelations from inside the game. "Quite Brilliant ★★★★★" - FourFourTwo magazine. "A footballing masterpiece... kept me sniggering and dribbling to and from work for the next week" - Beesotted magazine. "We hope Maurice Johnston has a sense of humour" - Matchday magazine. As serialised on Radio 5. The football cult book to end them all!

FOOTBALL AND THE COMMONS PEOPLE
edited by David Bull & Alastair Campbell
320pp A5 paperback ISBN 1 872204 05 8
£9.95 (+£1.50p&p/ Europe £3/ Rest £6)
30MPs and former MPs describe their experiences of, and opinions on, 'the people's game'. Serious issues such as Denis Howell on the politics of the '66 World Cup and David Evans justifying his policies as chairman of Luton Town and Maggie's lapdog! And fans-eye confessions: who indulged in the rather unparliamentary activity of "Taunting Rangers supporters" out of the car window (and not when he was a teenager either!). Was one MP really among the Tartan Horde ripping up Wembley in 1977? And which MP has an Irish Cup-Winner's medal - an Ulster Unionist playing for Derry City! Includes Roy Hattersley, Kenneth Clarke, Michael Howard, Michael Foot, Gordon Brown, Ann Taylor and more. Fascinating reading throughout.

EL TEL WAS A SPACE ALIEN
The Best Of The Alternative Football Press Vol. 1
edited by Martin Lacey
200pp A4 paperback ISBN 1 872204 00 7
£5.95 (+£1.50 p&p/ Europe £3/ Rest £6)
GET YOUR WRITS OUT
Another Dose Of The Alternative Football Press
edited by Martin Lacey
200pp A4 paperback ISBN 1 872204 02 3
£6.95 (+£1.50 p&p/ Europe £3/ Rest £6)
SPECIAL OFFER: Buy both the above for £10 post free (UK only)
Two classic compilations tracing the history and development of football fanzines, packed with features by, from and about the genre. Vol.1 covers the period from the conception of When Saturday Comes to the Hillsborough disaster. Vol.2 covers 1989-91. El Tel... was voted one of the ten most culturally significant sports books of the decade in Sportspages' 10th anniversary poll.

Juma
MAIL ORDER

Our mail order department can supply almost any British book in print, plus videos, audio and multimedia. Please enquire for more information. We are also commercial printers specialising in short-run books, magazines, catalogues etc. and will be please to quote for all your business printing requirements.

**Juma Printing & Publishing
Trafalgar Works, 44 Wellington Street
Sheffield S1 4HD
Tel. 0114 272 0915 Fax. 0114 278 6550
Email: MLacey5816@aol.com**